Workout
ADVANCED

WORKBOOK

Paul Radley

Kathy Burke

WORKOUT ADVANCED WORKBOOK

Pearson Education Limited.
Edinburgh Gate, Harlow,
Essex, CM20 2JE, England

© Paul Radley and Kathy Burke 1994

First published by Thomas Nelson and Sons Ltd 1994
This edition published by Addison Wesley Longman Ltd 1997
Fifth impression 1999

ISBN 0-17-556521-X

All rights reserved; no part of this publication may be reproduced, stored in a retrieval system, or transmitted in any form or by any means, electronic, mechanical, photocopying, recording or otherwise, without the prior written permission of the Publishers.

Printed in Malaysia, ACM

Acknowledgements

The publishers would like to thank all those who took part in recordings and supplied photographs, and are grateful to the following for permission to reproduce copyright material on the pages stated:

Faber & Faber Ltd: *We are Still Married* by Garrison Keillor, page 4
The Independent: David Bowen, page 6; Arabella Warner, page 49
BBC: page 10
HarperCollins Publishers Ltd: *Memories, Dreams and Reflections* by C G Jung, published by Fontana, page 10; *A Traveller's Life* by Eric Newby, page 24
Penguin Books: *Attacks of Opinion* by Terry Jones (Penguin Books 1988) © Terry Jones 1988, pages 11–12; *Games People Play* by Eric Berne (Penguin Books 1967, first published by Andre Deutsch) © Eric Berne 1964, pages 26–27; Desert War (page 20) from *True Tales* by David Day and Tony Husband (Pelham 1990) © David Day and Tony Husband 1990, page 41
Private Eye: pages 13, 21, 59
Hamish Hamilton/Penguin: reprinted by permission of the Peters, Fraser and Dunlop Group Ltd, page 16
Grub Street: pages 19, 76
Penguin Books (distributors): *Tunisia – The Rough Guide*, page 20, *Egypt – The Rough Guide*, page 93
British Airways Holidays: page 22
Hodder and Stoughton Ltd: *A Murder of Quality* by John le Carré, page 29
Options Magazine: © Arabella Warner, page 32
Chatta & Windus: *Cider with Rosie* by Laurie Lee, page 35
Virago Press: © Deborah Tannen, published by Virago Press 1992, page 35
House of Colour: page 41
The European: 'The Weekly Newspaper for Europe', page 43
Time Out: pages 55, 93
High Places Ltd: page 56
Allergan Ltd: page 56
Steel Hunter Ltd: reproduced by permission of J Barbour & Sons Ltd, South Shields. BARBOUR is a Registered Trade Mark. page 56
Haynes Publishing: reproduced with permission from the Haynes Moto Guzzi 750, 850 & 1000 V-Twins motorcycle manual, 1990, page 56

Mills & Boon Ltd: (producer and copyright holder) page 59
HarperCollins/Flamingo: The New Café from *London Observed: Stories and Sketches* by Doris Lessing. ©1990 Doris Lessing. Reprinted by permission of Jonathan Clowes Ltd., London, on behalf of Doris Lessing, pages 57–58.
She Magazine: Christina Konig, page 61
Sidgewick and Jackson: *Survivor* – The Authorised Biography of Eric Clapton/Ray Coleman, page 64
Random Century: Anne Tyler, page 66
Victor Gollancz: *Summerhill* by A S Neill, page 67
Jonathan Cape/Penguin Books Ltd: *Boy* by Roald Dahl, pages 67–68
Richard Ashwith: *The Observer* © published by permission of *The Observer* ©, page 69
E Jenkins: page 70
Sheil Land Associates Ltd: *The Fakes's Progress* by Tom Keating, Geraldine and Frank Norman, published by Hutchinson (Part I © Tom Keating and Frank Norman), pages 74–75

Every effort has been made to trace owners of copyright, but if any omissions can be rectified, the publishers will be pleased to make the necessary arrangements.

Photographs
Steve Benbow Photography: 8.1.
Allan Cash Photo Library: 7.3.
G. Galvin Photography: 13.3.
The Ronald Grant Archive/Cinema Museum: 13.2.
The Independent Newspaper: 1.2/Craig Easton 9.1.
The Kobal Collection: 11.1, 11.1b, 13.4.
The National Gallery: p14, 14.2.
Network Photographers/Abrahams: 6.1.
Paul Radley: 3.1, 4.2a, 4.23b, 14.1.
Rex Features: 1.1, 7.1, 7.2, 10.1.
The Science Photo Library: 2.1.
Tony Stone Worldwide: p39 ×3.

Illustrations
Harvey Collins, Sophie Grillet, Pantelis Palios, Nick Ward and Gecko Limited.

Contents

Unit 1	4
Unit 2	10
Unit 3	14
Unit 4	18
Unit 5	25
Unit 6	30
Unit 7	38
Unit 8	42
Unit 9	48
Unit 10	52
Unit 11	59
Unit 12	64
Unit 13	69
Unit 14	73
Tapescript of Student's Cassette	78
Answer Key	84

Unit 1

Vocabulary development — humour

1 Without looking at page 6 of your Students' Book, write six words which describe types of humour.

1 _____ 4 _____
2 _____ 5 _____
3 _____ 6 _____

Now write three words or phrases which describe how funny something was. Include a modifier with each word or phrase.

1 _____
2 _____
3 _____

Now write one idiom related to laughter.

_____

Vocabulary building — adjectives ending in -y

-y combines with nouns to form adjectives, for example *dirt* (n) + *-y* makes *dirty* (adj). Adjectives formed in this way express 'characterisation' by the thing the noun refers to. For example, if something is *dirty*, it is covered with dirt; a *smoky* room is one that is full of smoke.

2 How are these nouns converted?

1 Nouns ending in -e.
2 One-syllable nouns ending in -b, -d, -g, -n or -t preceded by a single vowel.

Form adjectives from these nouns:

cloud _____   fog _____
rain _____   sun _____
thirst _____   mud _____

Now think of and write six other adjectives ending in *-y* and the nouns which they are derived from.

1 _____ 4 _____
2 _____ 5 _____
3 _____ 6 _____

Listening

Garrison Keillor is the best-selling author of *Lake Wobegon Days*, *Happy to be Here* and *Leaving Home*. He was born in Minnesota in 1942 and graduated from the University of Minnesota in 1966. He is married to Ulla Skaerved, and they have four children. From 1974 to 1987 he was host of the popular live radio show, *A Prairie Home Companion*. In this recording he reads an extract called 'After the Fall' from his book, *We are Still Married*.

3 Before you listen
Think. Have you ever had an embarrassing experience in public? Like falling over or walking into a door? How did you feel? Who saw what happened? Why was the experience embarrassing?

4 ⟦S1⟧ While you listen
Read these descriptions of events.

1 ☐ The man came out of his house and fell down the steps, landing on his back.
2 ☐ The man came out of his house, walked into a tree and fell over.
3 ☐ A passer-by asked him if he was okay.
4 ☐ A postwoman who saw what had happened started laughing at him.
5 ☐ The man got up and went back into the house.
6 ☐ The woman helped him get back into the house.
7 ☐ He told his wife about the fall.
8 ☐ He described how he felt about the fall.
9 ☐ The man's son had laughed at him when he had fallen over a few months before.
10 ☐ The man had laughed at his son falling on dog droppings a few months before.

Now listen and tick the events which Garrison Keillor describes in the extract.

Unit 1

5 [S1] Listening and note-taking
Read this list of categories.

The author's description of a person's initial reaction after falling over.

His conversation with the woman who saw the incident.

His description of the woman.

His impression of the woman's real feelings.

The incident with his son.

His conversation with his son after the incident.

His conclusion about such incidents.

Now listen to the cassette again. Make notes about each category.

Idioms laugh

6
On page 6 of your Students' Book you learned four idioms connected with laughing and joking. Tick the correct alternative in each case to make idioms related to laughter.

1 You (a) die ☐ (b) are ☐ (c) stand ☐ laughing – you've got a good job and an excellent salary and you only have to work three days a week.

2 The boss has given Jim next week off and we all wanted that week, but when he finds out what the weather forecast is like he'll be laughing on the other (a) part ☐ (b) half ☐ (c) side ☐ of his face.

3 Although she lost a lot of money in the stock market crash, Jenny tried to laugh it (a) off ☐ (b) away ☐ (c) down ☐.

4 Ann's laughing all the way to the (a) club ☐ (b) pub ☐ (c) bank ☐ – when she bought her house everyone advised her to wait until prices went down. In fact, they have gone up fifteen per cent in two years.

5 They gave Jeremy five thousand pounds when they made him redundant. He had the (a) ultimate ☐ (b) last ☐ (c) final ☐ laugh, though – the firm went bankrupt a year later and the rest of the staff got nothing.

Pronunciation vowels and spelling

7 [S2]
You may sometimes find it difficult to pronounce a word from its spelling. English vowels are sometimes not pronounced as they are written. Listen and repeat these words.

1 /iː/ ski   encyclopaedia   analyses   ceiling   key
2 /ɪ/ movies   orange   mountain   village   pretty   started   wicked   supposedly
3 /e/ many   leisure   leopard   friend
4 /æ/ passion   plaid
5 /ɑː/ demand   ask   aunt   clerk   reservoir   heart
6 /ɒ/ sausage   rendezvous   gone   cough   knowledge
7 /ɔː/ broad   door   restore   drawer
8 /ʊ/ full   push   cook   would   woman
9 /uː/ do   move   shoe   rheumatism   two
10 /ʌ/ come   mother   couple   flood   does

8 [S2]
Which of the groups above does each of these words belong to?
Write the number in the box.

Example: a floor 7

b litre ☐   f Gloucester ☐
c image ☐   g pudding ☐
d southern ☐   h sergeant ☐
e who ☐   i says ☐

Listen and check your answers.

Now listen and repeat.

Unit 1

Reading

9 British people often have bizarre hobbies which others find difficult to understand. For example, 'bashers' are railway enthusiasts who spend their spare time following a single locomotive round the country. The 'bashers' themselves have difficulty explaining exactly why! The British also like collecting things. Read Part 1 of the text quickly and find out about David Bowen's bizarre collection.

...Sickbags by the dozen

David Bowen lays his motion discomfort bags on the table

PART 1
THE *Independent on Sunday*'s industrial editor, David Bowen, collects airline sick-bags. He started about 10 years ago when he used to travel extensively, but now the collection has its own momentum. "I get sent several bags a month,' he says. "All my friends know that I collect these things, and they mention it to their friends. Then when any of them go on flights, they stare ahead of them for hours on end and sooner or later remember to pick one up.'

He now has about 400 bags covering about 200 airlines: they are displayed all over the walls of his house. He asks people to pick up a couple so that he has a swap although, he says, "there is a slightly limited market: my only real trading partner is a German who I met in Jordan eight years ago'.

PART 2 The bags, Bowen says, say a lot about the ___1___ of origin. Far Eastern ones tend to be lavish and ___2___, Germanic ones are severely practical, eastern European ones ___3___ "the shortage of decent paper".

"___4___ US airlines manage to combine their passion for euphemism with good American commercial ___5___," he says. "Passengers on American Airlines are ___6___ to put their films into their motion discomfort bags, ___7___. TWA has a developing offer one side and a gin rummy score card on the other.' His ___8___ comes from Air Afrique, which has a picture of a woman giving birth.

Bowen is ___9___ to hear from anyone who ___10___ to join the bag bartering system. The hobby is not ___11___ developed to have monetary values attached to it, but the schoolboy swap system should ___12___ well. "___13___ you, if someone came up with a pre-War bag, maybe from Imperial Airways, I would very ___14___ think about letting them have several, maybe ___15___ the Air Afrique one."

© *The Independent*

10 Read Part 2 of the text. Circle the best word for each space.

Example: 1 (country) airline company artist

2 strange cheap exotic enormous
3 demonstrate reflect contain lack
4 Several All No The
5 feeling sense business knowledge
6 told asked encouraged instructed
7 so but then while
8 favourite preferred biggest beloved
9 proud keen enthusiastic desperate
10 likes needs wants prefers
11 enough thoroughly totally sufficiently
12 work function happen go
13 Listen Think Mind Do
14 hopefully often likely seriously
15 even also too not

Phrasal verbs up

11 Find the phrasal verbs in the text that correspond to these definitions.

to obtain or acquire casually _____

to produce or find _____

These two phrasal verbs have many other meanings. Complete these sentences with the appropriate verb.

1 I hadn't considered Wilkins for the job until his name _____ up in a meeting about sales figures last week.

2 With Christmas _____ up soon, most people are thinking about what to give their family and friends.

3 She left the restaurant before the end of the meal leaving us to _____ up the bill.

4 I'm sorry, but I can't go out with you this evening; something's _____ up at work.

5 People are afraid of _____ up hitchhikers these days.

6 When I applied for this job, I didn't know that a better one would _____ up in London.

7 She _____ up a working knowledge of Arabic when she was living in Saudi.

8 He was stopped by the police for drunken driving; his case _____ up at Marylebone Magistrates' Court next week.

9 I _____ up my car for three hundred pounds at an auction in Hampshire.

10 She _____ him up in a pub on the Great West Road and they went back to his house.

Grammar the present

12 Match the functions listed below to these sentences. Write the letter(s) of the appropriate function(s) in the box(es) next to each sentence.

1 The book I'm reading at the moment is about a Los Angeles policeman who investigates a series of bank robberies carried out by an ex-car thief and his two Mexican accomplices. ☐

2 I'm living in a small flat in the centre of town at the moment. ☐

3 I'm a writer and I work at home most of the time. ☐

4 To get to my house you can get a train to the nearest town and then you take the Number 23 bus and get off at the hospital. ☐

5 More and more people in this country are selling their cars and using public transport. ☐

A general truths
B moment of speaking
C general time (habits/states)
D dramatic narrative
E synopses of books/films, etc.
F temporary situations
G commentaries
H instructions
I progressive change

Now change the information in the sentences to make them true for you.

13 Correct these statements and complete them with the appropriate form of the verbs in brackets.

Example: The sun (rise) __rises__ in the ~~west~~ east and (set) __sets__ in the west.

1 The earth (rotate) _____ in an anti-clockwise direction.

2 When cold air (rise) _____ it (get) _____ hotter.

3 The sea (rise) _____ and (fall) _____ according to the phases of the sun.

4 A lunar eclipse (occur) _____ when the moon (pass) _____ between the sun and the earth.

5 Water (boil) _____ at a temperature of 80 degrees centigrade.

14 Complete this joke using verbs from the box in the appropriate form.

| follow overtake drive look stop see answer |
| get wind reply say slow come check |

This man _____ along a country road one day when he _____ in his rear-view mirror and _____ a police car following him. He _____ his speed and _____ down but the police car still _____ him. After another mile the police car _____ him and _____ him. The policeman _____ out and _____ up to the car. The man _____ down the window and _____, 'Can I help you, Officer?' and the policeman _____, 'We picked up a woman a mile or two back who claims to be your wife. She says that she fell out of your car.' And the man _____, 'Oh, thank goodness for that! I thought I'd gone deaf!'

Unit 1

Writing — formal letters

15 Look at this letter from a bank to one of its customers. There are mistakes in the layout and the style is inappropriate for a formal letter. Rewrite the letter.

```
                    Paul Miller           Joe Hillier
                    88 Aberdeen Road      TSB Bank
                    Kensington            PO Box 397
                    London                London
                    W8 31Y                NW6 3JJ

        22/12/92

        Dear Paul,

        Thanks for your cheque book application.

        I've had a look in the files and guess what?,
        we sent you a cheque book in June. No one's
        used any of the cheques yet so let us know if
        you got the cheque book or not. Get in touch
        asap if you didn't get it so I can get it
        stopped and send you a new one.

        There should also be an application for
        Eurocheques in this letter, if my secretary
        hasn't forgotten to put it in! Fill it in and
        send it back to me.

        A bientôt, as the French say,

        Cheers,

        Joe
```

See the Answer Key for the correct version of the letter.

Improve your language learning — extensive reading

> **Intensive reading** is the sort of reading you do in class, where you study a text in detail, looking up unknown words and doing comprehension tasks. **Extensive reading**, on the other hand, is the reading you do unsupervised outside the classroom.

Which of these statements do you agree and disagree with? Write *A* or *D*.

1. ☐ I should keep a dictionary at hand to look up words I don't know, when I come across them.
2. ☐ Newspapers and magazines are the most useful source of extensive reading material.
3. ☐ The grammatical accuracy of my English may improve through reading extensively.
4. ☐ The best novels to read are the great classics of literature like the novels of Jane Austen and Charles Dickens.
5. ☐ I should try to read part of an English newspaper or book at least once a month.
6. ☐ I can expect to increase my vocabulary by reading outside class.
7. ☐ 'Readers' specifically written for English language students are a waste of time.
8. ☐ It's important to build up my reading speed if I am to make progress.

Now read the following paragraphs. They comment on the statements above. Compare your reactions.

1. D Using a dictionary while you are reading extensively is not really necessary. It can even be counterproductive. You may lose interest in what you are reading if you are constantly stopping to look up words. It is better to carry on reading and try to work out the meaning from context.

2. D Not necessarily. One advantage of newspapers and magazines is that they are probably more readily available in your country than books (see Note 1 below). It's a good idea to subscribe to a magazine related to one of your leisure interests – finding out new information may motivate you to read in English.

8

3 ▢A Yes! Coming across the grammatical structures that you have studied in your lessons in an authentic context will consolidate your knowledge of them, even though you may not be aware that this is happening.

4 ▢D Although you may enjoy reading the classics, you may find the style and vocabulary difficult and unfamiliar (see Note 2 below).

5 ▢D No, more. Reading once a month is not really enough if you want to make rapid progress. It's a good idea to read a magazine or newspaper at least once a week and novels as often as you can.

6 ▢A Yes, you probably will increase your vocabulary if you read challenging material regularly.

7 ▢− This is a matter of opinion. Some teachers believe that readers are more appropriate for the lower levels of language learning. Others don't believe in using them at all and encourage their students to get to grips with 'real' novels as early as possible. Try one and decide for yourself.

8 ▢D People read at different speeds both in their own and in foreign languages. Unless you need to read fast for your work or study or for an examination, speed is not important.

Notes

1 If your local newsagent doesn't stock foreign language newspapers and magazines, you could ask him or her to order one for you. Otherwise you can write to the subscriptions department of the publication and order direct by post.

2 Many bookshops now stock English language books or can be encouraged to start doing so. Alternatively, join a cultural organisation, such as the USIS (United States Information Service) or the British Council, which usually have a lending library.

You will be happiest reading the sort of things that you would read in your own language. Below are the opening lines of six books. Which one(s) would you like to go on reading?

A

Polly Alter used to like men, but she didn't trust them any more, or have very much to do with them. Last month, on her thirty-ninth birthday, it suddenly hit her that – though she hadn't planned it that way – almost all her dealings were with women. Her doctor, her dentist, her accountant, her therapist, her bank manager, and all her close friends were female.

B

Cannery Row in Monterey in California is a poem, a stink, a grating noise, a quality of light, a tone, a habit, a nostalgia, a dream. Cannery Row is the gathered and scattered, tin and iron and rust and splintered wood, chipped pavement and weedy lots and junk heaps, sardine canneries or corrugated iron, honky-tonks, restaurants and whore-houses, and little crowded groceries, and laboratories and flop-houses.

C

She closed the door behind her, and then it was quite silent, quite dark. She stood, and she could smell very faintly the dry smell of the bracken, coming over the common. Everything was dry now, for three weeks the sun had shone. It tired her, but throughout April and May, it had rained, and that, too, had been tiring, the endless, dull pattering on to the cottage roof.

D

The new curate seemed quite a nice young man, but what a pity it was that his combinations showed, tucked carelessly into his socks, when he sat down. Belinda had noticed it when they had met him for the first time at the vicarage last week and had felt quite embarrassed.

E

If you really want to hear about it, the first thing you'll probably want to know is where I was born, and what my lousy childhood was like, and how my parents were occupied and all before they had me, and all that David Copperfield kind of crap, but I don't feel like going into it.

F

The night Vincent was shot he saw it coming. The guy approached out of the streetlight on the corner of Meridian and Sixteenth, South Beach, and reached Vincent as he was walking from his car to his apartment building. It was early, a few minutes past nine.

Unit 2

Vocabulary development — the press

1 Use these sequences of words to make sentences about the press.

1 editor/newspaper/leader/comment
2 critic/review/arts
3 editor/sub-editor/reporter/photographer/designer
4 tabloid/newspaper/sensationalism/invasion of privacy/bad taste
5 quality/newspaper/articles/home/foreign/politics/sport

Vocabulary building — words ending in -ity

> -ity combines with some adjectives to form nouns which refer to the state or condition described by the adjective. For example, *equality* is the state of being equal; *anonymity* is the state of being anonymous.
> There are some words which do not follow this pattern, for example *locality*.

2 Put the words below into two lists: those which follow the *equality* pattern (List A) and those which don't (List B).

morality	sensitivity	simplicity
personality	superiority	publicity
security	majority	principality
brutality	minority	priority
familiarity	generosity	formality

Listening — the news

3 [S3] Listen to the radio news. Match the numbers to the information.

```
5        time of the news broadcast
90       date of the news broadcast
130      length in hours of an operation
200      number of people killed by a typhoon
26       percentage of properties destroyed by a typhoon
133      number of people missing or dead
6        speed of winds in miles per hour
1600     number of British athletes tested for drug abuse
2.5      age of the person operated on
8        number of times they postponed the operation
```

4 [S3] Now listen to the tape again. Make notes about each news story.
Write a sentence summarising each story, and include the information given in Exercise 3.

Pronunciation — th

5 Write **1** if *th* is voiced and **2** if it is unvoiced in the boxes under these words.

The three thousand soldiers thought they were saved.
☐ ☐ ☐   ☐ ☐

The sixth policeman threatened the safety of thousands.
☐ ☐   ☐   ☐ ☐

Through thick and thin Cyril taught them theology.
☐ ☐ ☐   ☐ ☐

Throughout the centuries these theories have thrived.
☐ ☐   ☐ ☐ ☐

[S4] Now listen to the sentences. Listen and repeat several times, increasing your speed each time until you can say the sentences as fast as the recorded version.

Grammar — narrative tenses

6 Complete this account of a dream from the case histories of the psychologist, Carl Gustav Jung, using the appropriate form of the verbs in brackets.

There is, for example, the case of the theologian which I (describe) _____ in 'Archetypes of the Collective Unconscious'. He (have) _____ a certain dream that he (stand) _____ on a slope from which he (have) _____ a beautiful view of a low valley covered with dense woods. In the dream he (know) _____ that in the middle of the woods there (be) _____ a lake, and he also (know) _____ that hitherto something (prevent) _____ always _____ him from going there. But this time he (want) _____ to carry out his plan. As he (approach) _____ the lake, the atmosphere (grow) _____ uncanny, and suddenly a light gust of wind (pass) _____ over the surface of the water, which (ripple) _____ darkly. He (awake) _____ with a cry of terror.

Unit 2

7 Use the table to make eight true sentences about yourself.

Examples: By the time I was eighteen I had been studying English for six years.
At eight o'clock this morning I was having a coffee.

By the time		was	five ten eighteen fifteen twenty	I	started school. smoked a cigarette. learned to drive a car. had a part-time job		
In 1990 At eight o'clock this morning At this time last week Last weekend When I started this course At the beginning of this year	I				been living in this town living in a different house still at school studying English having breakfast. sleeping. having a coffee. travelling to work. studied. went to the cinema. visited friends. stayed at home.	for	six ten fifteen	years.

The middle column for the second row reads: had / had been / was / (nothing)

Reading

This article is one of a series written for a regular column in the *Guardian* newspaper by the writer and actor, Terry Jones.

8 Quickly read the first five paragraphs of the article and put them in the correct order. Write a number in the box.

Thirty Years On

A □
The one factor which was entirely new in human experience, and whose cancer-forming properties were only just beginning to be recognized, was exposure to certain forms of atomic radiation.

B □
I seem to remember all through the sixties and seventies people becoming increasingly alarmed by the huge increase in deaths from cancers. Cancer was dubbed the Modern Plague, and the medical profession was just as baffled by what was causing it as their medieval counterparts had been by the Black Death.

C □
The so-called 'safe levels' recommended by such bodies as the National Radiological Protection Board are not actually 'safe levels' at all, but just rough guesses as to how many people will die as a result of a given level of radiation, and what number of such deaths can be considered socially acceptable (by the NRPB), given the enormous benefits of nuclear power and the increasing importance of nuclear reactors as tourist attractions.

D □
Until recently our estimates of how much radiation human beings can be exposed to had been based on the data provided by the Hiroshima and Nagasaki experiments. However, it is now clear that these estimates grossly underrated the problem, and that, in fact, no level of exposure to radiation is safe – especially since some human beings appear to be more susceptible than others.

E
Back in the fourteenth century one of the favourite theories was that the Plague was caused by a poisonous cloud that had swept over the earth from China. In the sixties and seventies nobody was looking at 'poisonous clouds', but practically every other aspect of modern life fell under suspicion and was investigated.

9 Now read the paragraphs more carefully and answer these questions.

1 What is the central topic of the article?
2 Why does the writer mention the Black Death?
3 What does he say about 'safe levels' of radiation?

Unit 2

10 Read the rest of the article below and answer these questions.

1 What does Terry Jones suggest may have been one cause of the increase in the number of cancers in the sixties and seventies?

2 How did the government deal with the 1957 Windscale disaster?

3 How has the nuclear power industry reacted to accusations that nuclear power is unsafe?

Last week marked the thirtieth anniversary of the 1957 Windscale disaster, when a major fire in the reactor sent a radioactive cloud drifting – not out to sea, as the Atomic Energy Authority claimed at the time – but south-east across most of England. To celebrate the event, the Public Records Office released some (not all) of the top-secret documents that reveal just how bad the disaster was, and just how far those running the country and the industry were prepared to lie through their teeth about it. Far from being a harmless inconvenience, which simply involved throwing a lot of milk down the drain, it now turns out that the 1957 Windscale disaster was far worse than the meltdown at Three Mile Island in 1979, which has since brought the development of nuclear power in the USA to a virtual standstill. Windscale 1957 was more on a par with Chernobyl 1986, and one independent expert (Dr Gofman, Professor Emeritus at the University of California) has estimated that Chernobyl will produce 424,300 cancers in the Soviet Union and 526,700 elsewhere in Europe.

So I wonder how much time and money was wasted in the sixties and seventies, searching for the causes of the Modern Plague, when one very obvious possible cause was, indeed, a poisonous cloud – but one that was brazenly lied out of existence by both the government and the nuclear power industry.

Even last week, I actually heard a spokesman for British Nuclear Fuels Ltd saying on TV: 'Not a single person has ever been killed in a nuclear accident in this country.' It's rather like a spokesman for the motor industry saying that nobody has ever yet been killed on British roads by driving a car … Well, it's true! Each year over 5,000 may get killed when their cars hit trees or go under lorries or when they're run over by other people's cars, but no one yet has ever been killed by grasping the steering wheel or by changing gear.

I suppose BNFL is forced to rely on such transparent sophistry because its record is actually the total opposite of what it claims it to be. The nuclear power industry is dangerous, dirty, dear and – as last week's revelations demonstrate beyond all doubt – downright dishonest.

(by Terry Jones)

---

11 Read the whole article again and underline all the words connected with nuclear energy.

12 Complete these sentences with some of the words that you have underlined in the article.

1 The effects of long-term exposure to _____ are quite frightening, and often include cancer and premature death.

2 Nuclear _____ of the type which caused the Chernobyl disaster are still in use in parts of the former Soviet Union.

3 The Irish Sea has been polluted for many years by the dumping of _____ waste.

4 A _____ can occur when the core of a nuclear power plant overheats uncontrollably.

Idioms `teeth`

> In the article 'Thirty Years On' the expression *to lie through their teeth* is used. This is an informal expression which means 'to tell deliberate lies'.

13 Read these sentences which contain more idioms using the word *tooth* or *teeth*.

1 I'm *fed up to the back teeth* with people complaining.

2 I know it's a lot of work but I like a job I can *get my teeth into*.

3 The proposed new motorway would go right past her house. She will *fight tooth and nail* to stop it.

Rewrite the sentences. Keep the same meaning, but use your own words in place of the expressions in italics.

Phrasal verbs `turn`

> In the article the verb *turn* is used with the particle *out* to mean 'happen in a particular way'.

14 Which phrasal verbs with *turn* have these meanings?

1 stop and return to the place you started travelling from _____

2 refuse a request or offer _____

3 go to bed _____

4 stop being excited or interested _____

5 arrive somewhere unexpectedly _____

Now write sentences to show the meaning of each verb.

Unit 2

Grammar `noun phrases`

> Look at this noun phrase from the article about paparazzi on page 16 of the Students' Book:
> ... Jean-Claude Ratteuil, a wily Frenchman who works the French Riviera, specialising in the Monacan royal family.

15 Now write similar noun phrases, including at least one qualifier and one modifier to describe the following:

1 yourself
2 your family
3 your town
4 your area
5 your English teacher
6 your English class
7 your English school
8 your country

Example: (yourself) *a forty-year-old Swede living abroad*

Writing `small ads`

16 Read the small ads from *Private Eye*'s 'Eye Let' column and make notes about the suitability of each property. Choose one of the ads and write a letter asking for more information – availability, cost to rent, and so on.

17 Now write your own ad offering your house or flat for rent. Follow the style of the *Private Eye* column.

MY CYPRUS VILLA sleeps 6–9, rental £150 pw. For the adventurous/independent types. Superb sea and mountain views. Phone/fax 0923 267213 for leaflet.

BEAUTIFULLY SITUATED clifftop Edwardian holiday home – overlooks sea and sandy beaches on Cornwall's Roseland peninsula. Sleeps 8-plus. First two weeks July, last week September still available, plus other dates throughout year. Phone 042-482 404.

SUMMER IN SOMERSET? House (1 double, 1 single bedroom) to let in mystical Glastonbury's town centre. Centrally-heated, fully furnished and with all necessary utensils, crockery etc. Telephone: 0234 211606 (answerphone) for leaflet. (Festival week still available!)

FRANCE – TO LET, holiday flatlet near Montpelier. £110 weekly. Tel. 010 33 67 44 28 21.

Extension and consolidation

Editing

1 This is the first part of a newspaper article about phoney policemen. There is a word missing in every line of the text. Put asterisks (*) in the text to show where the words are missing and write the words in the spaces below.

Britain's first robot policeman was unveiled yesterday the West Mercia force. SAM (Speed and Aggression Moderator), was holding a radar gun, could eventually appear kerbsides to deter speeding motorists. SAM is five foot seven and half inches tall, wears a uniform and has a papier-mâché head turns slowly, powered a small battery-charged engine.
Chief Supt Brian Humphreys, West Mercia's head traffic, said: 'SAM moves faster than real thing.'
The robot went on show the launch of the force's new offensive against aggressive drivers. Public reaction the idea of sending SAM on the beat will be gauged displaying him at exhibitions.

1 _____   7 _____
2 _____   8 _____
3 _____   9 _____
4 _____   10 _____
5 _____   11 _____
6 _____

Dictation

2 Look at this gapped version of the rest of the article. Try to fill in the gaps. Use a pencil.

Cardboard policemen have _____ been used to _____ shoplifting in supermarkets, _____ full-sized cardboard patrol _____ have been placed _____ motorway bridges. But _____ fear that SAM _____ be targeted by _____ if left alone _____ duty by the _____ .

Mr Humphreys said, '_____ a futuristic model _____ could well become _____ second generation of _____ cardboard or plastic _____ . The concept is _____ same – people see _____ policeman and they _____ .'

[S5] Now listen to a recording of the text. Complete the text with the original words.

Unit 3

Vocabulary development — life choices

1 Without looking at your Students' Book, write four words related to security and stability and four words related to adventure and excitement.

Security/stability
1 _____
2 _____
3 _____
4 _____

Adventure/excitement
5 _____
6 _____
7 _____
8 _____

2 Now use the words to write six sentences about sports, hobbies and lifestyles which are either very secure or very exciting.

Vocabulary building — nouns ending in -ance

-ance combines with some verbs to form nouns which refer to the action, process or state indicated by the verb. For example, *admittance* is the act of entering a place or being allowed to enter it; *observance* is the process of observing something.

Spelling note: a final *-ate* is replaced by *-ance*.

-ance replaces *-ant* at the end of some adjectives to form nouns which refer to the state or quality described by the adjective. For example, *arrogance* is the quality of being arrogant; *elegance* is the quality of being elegant.

3 Write the original adjectives or verbs from which these nouns are formed. Put *a* for *adjective* or *v* for *verb* in the box next to each word. Three of the nouns do not fit either of the categories described above – mark them with a cross (x).

Example:
insignificance ___insignificant___ [a]

renaissance _____ ☐
grievance _____ ☐
brilliance _____ ☐
maintenance _____ ☐
intolerance _____ ☐
reluctance _____ ☐
entrance _____ ☐
disturbance _____ ☐
accordance _____ ☐
appliance _____ ☐
disappearance _____ ☐

4 Complete these sentences with the correct nouns from the list above.

1 The cause of the plane crash in the Alps yesterday has been attributed to poor _____.

2 The main _____ of the National Gallery in London is in Trafalgar Square.

3 Racial _____ is often at the root of violence in that area.

4 The government showed some _____ to support the military measures required to solve the problem.

5 Carson McCullers was a writer of great _____ although unfortunately not many people have read her work.

6 Gas _____ must always be installed on an outside wall otherwise they may be dangerous.

Unit 3

Listening

5 [S6] Read the statements below carefully. Listen to Sarah-Jane talking about her cycling trip to Spain. Decide which statements are true and which are false.

1. [F] Sarah-Jane has never been on a holiday where she has spent her time lying on the beach.
2. [F] It was Sarah-Jane's idea to go on a cycling holiday.
3. [F] At the beginning of the holiday they travelled with their bicycles on the train.
4. [ ] They met a lot of Spanish people when they were travelling by car.
5. [T] Sarah-Jane thinks it's a waste of time to travel by car in the mountains.
6. [T] Spanish people like cyclists a lot.
7. [F] When they were shot at, Sarah-Jane and Nigel knew they were in a hunting area.
8. [F] Their tent was damaged in the incident.

6 [S6] Listen again and write a sentence saying why each statement in Exercise 5 is true or false.

Example: 1 *False. She says it has been a long time since she has been on a beach holiday, not that she has never been on one.*

7 Make a list of the advantages that Sarah-Jane mentions of a cycling holiday compared with a traditional beach holiday.

Idioms `heart`

In the article on page 19 of your Students' Book the expression *at heart* is used in the sentence *but it was all foolishness and at heart I think I knew it*. In this context *at heart* means 'in reality'.

8 Here are some more idioms using the word *heart*. Match them to the explanations.

1. after one's own heart
2. by heart
3. have one's heart in one's mouth
4. wear one's heart on one's sleeve
5. set one's heart on
6. from the bottom of one's heart
7. take to heart
8. to one's heart's content
9. with all one's heart

A show one's feelings openly
B very sincerely or deeply
C appealing to one's own tastes
D take seriously or be upset about
E be full of apprehension or excitement
F very willingly
G have as one's ambition to obtain
H by committing to memory
I as much as one wishes

Pronunciation

`weak forms – the five prepositions`

9 Look at the prepositions in these sentences. Underline the ones you expect to take their weak form.

1. They'll be **at** the office **at** the weekend too.
2. Alice comes **from** New York but I've no idea where Geoff comes **from**.
3. This was the first **of** five courses that he was going **to** attend.
4. I don't know what this is **for**. You'd better have a look **at** the instructions.
5. She's been working **for** the Ministry **of** Defence **for** six years now.
6. During their holiday in Spain they were shot **at**!

[S7] Now listen to the sentences and check your answers.

Listen again and repeat.

Unit 3

Reading

One morning in June 1977, (1) _____. The Triumph had stopped protesting and was running freely. All my equipment was in working order. I sat in the saddle with the same ease that others find in an armchair, and could maintain that position comfortably for twelve hours or more. I was very light, some thirty pounds below the weight I set out at four years earlier, but my body functioned better than ever except in one respect: (2) _____. To read a telephone directory in twilight I needed glasses. I still smoked cigarettes, and still wished I didn't.

I was carrying rice from Iran, raisins and dried mulberries from Afghanistan, tea from Assam, curry spices from Calcutta, stock cubes from Greece, halva from Turkey and some soya sauce from Penang.

In a polythene screwtop bottle, bought from a shop in Kathmandu, was the rest of the sesame seed oil I had bought in Boddghaya. The rice and the raisins were in plastic boxes from Guatemala. My teapot was bought at Victoria Falls, and (3) _____. A small box of henna leaves from the Sudan, a vial of rose water from Peshawar and some silver ornaments from Ootacamund were all tucked into a Burmese lacquered bowl. This in turn sat inside a Russian samovar from Kabul.

My leather tank bags and saddle cover were made in Argentina. The tent and sleeping bag were original from London, (4) _____. I had a blanket from Peru and a hammock from Brazil. I was still wearing Lulu's silver necklace and an elephant hair bracelet from Kenya. The Australian fishing rod was where the sword from Cairo had once sat, and an umbrella from Thailand replaced the one I had lost in Argentina.

By far the most valuable of all my possessions was a Kashmiri carpet, a lovely thing smothered in birds and animals to a Shiraz design, (5) _____.

I came down through Lyons and stayed off the motorway, crossing the Rhône at St Esprit and heading off for Nîmes. I was still playing that clip of film in my head: the avenue, the plane trees, the sun flicking between the trunks and leaves. (6) _____. I would be riding up that avenue, and by that single act I would be sealing off for ever the four most eventful years of my life.

(7) _____.

It should have been intolerable. I should have turned and fled the other way. It was after all a kind of death. The only Ted Simon I knew was the one who moved on. The Hello-Goodbye Man. (8) _____. Half man, half bike: if not Jupiter, then Pegasus, perhaps, or at least a Centaur.

But soon, no more. I would take my things off my bike and put them away in cupboards. I would wear ordinary clothes. And this bike, which had been 63,400 miles round the world, I would ride to the shops. And most of my days, from then on, (9) _____. Yes, it would be a bit like death, but I welcomed it. I rode on through the sunshine until I came to the avenue, (10) _____.

10 Look at this page from the final part of Ted Simon's book, *Travels with Jupiter*. Several sentences or parts of sentences are missing. They are listed below. Match them to the gaps.

A I would spend trying to remember.

B but the bag had been refilled with down in San Francisco.

C Any minute now . . . The End.

D my right eye was less efficient after the accident in Penang.

E but it would have been hard to say which of my possessions was the most precious.

F From person to person, country to country, continent to continent.

G I rode over the Jura Mountains into France.

H and the sun flickered through the plane trees exactly as I had remembered.

I my enamel plates were made in China and inherited from Bruno at La Plata.

J Within hours, even within a modest number of minutes, the film would merge with reality.

11 Which of the following best describes how Ted Simon felt as he neared the end of his journey? Tick the appropriate box.

1 ☐ Fed up with the journey and desperate to get back home.

2 ☐ A mixture of happiness to be home and sorrow that his journey was over.

3 ☐ A fear of the journey being over, nearly as strong as the fear of death.

4 ☐ Relief that the journey was over and excitement at the prospect of starting another journey.

Write a sentence giving evidence to support your answer.

Unit 3

Phrasal verbs — get

> In the extract from *Travels with Jupiter* on page 19 of your Students' Book you read how Ted Simon *got on* the bike and set off in the general direction of the English Channel.
> If you *get on* something, you move your body so that you are sitting, standing or lying on it.

12 The phrasal verb *get on* has many other meanings. Close your Workbook and write sentences demonstrating as many meanings as you can think of.

13 Look at these explanations of the various meanings of the verb *get on*. Write a sentence for any of the meanings which you didn't include in your list in Exercise 12.

1 If you get on a bus, train or plane, you get into it.
2 If you get on the telephone to someone, you talk to them on the telephone.
3 If you get a piece of clothing on, you dress yourself in it.
4 If you get on with an activity, you start doing it or continue doing it.
5 If you ask how someone is getting on with an activity, you are asking about their progress.
6 If you get on in your career, you are successful.
7 To get on without someone or something means to manage to continue or succeed without them.
8 If you get on with someone, you like them and have a friendly relationship with them.
9 If someone gets on a committee or a television or radio programme, they are successful in being accepted to take part in it.
10 If you say that someone is getting on, you mean that they are old.
11 If you say that time is getting on, you mean that there is not much time left before something is expected to happen or before something must be done.

Grammar — past simple, present perfect and present perfect continuous

14 Correct the mistakes in the verb tenses in these sentences.

1 They have been living in London for ten years and they left three years ago.
2 I worked for the organisation Shelter since 1989.
3 Have you been seeing the latest Eric Rohmer film?
4 She has been to Namibia three years ago.
5 George? No, sorry, he just went out.
6 Did you ever play squash before or is this the first time?

15 Use these verbs to write nine statements about yourself. Use each tense three times.

| study | live | visit | go | read | see | write | eat | work |

Example: study   I have been studying English for eight years.
         or   I studied French when I was at school.

Writing — composition

16 Look at these two composition titles.

A Dangerous sports should be banned
B Regionalism is a dangerous phenomenon

Look at the notes for the two compositions. They are mixed up. Separate the two sets of notes and choose one of the topics to write about. Use the notes to plan and then write your composition, adding any arguments of your own.

accidents always happen – the whole is more than the sum of its parts – life too boring otherwise – protect people from themselves – expensive for the state – national governments too far from people – regionalism is a form of racism – regionalism leads to wars – hurt only themselves – regional parties have no sound national policies – people need to take risks – innocent people sometimes hurt – some regions have been neglected by government – freedom of individual essential – regionalism conserves regional culture – different regions have different mentalities

Unit 4

Vocabulary development — another country

1 What practical and cultural problems can people expect to encounter when they arrive in the country you are living in at the moment? Make a list.

Write a sentence giving advice about ways of getting round each of the problems you list.

Example: Finding accommodation in London – Buy a London newspaper like 'Loot' as soon as it comes out and look at the small ads for flat-shares.

Vocabulary building — adjectives ending in -ing and -ed

> Present participles of transitive verbs used as adjectives describe the effect that something has on someone's feelings and ideas. For example, if you find something *disgusting*, it disgusts you. Present participles of intransitive verbs used as adjectives describe a continuing process or state. For example, a *recurring* problem is one that happens again and again.
>
> Past participles of transitive verbs used as adjectives indicate that something has been affected in some way. For example, *cook – cooked meat*; *excite – excited children*. Past participles of a few intransitive verbs are used as adjectives to indicate that a person or thing has done something. For example, a *retired* person is someone who has retired.
>
> *-ed* combines with some nouns to form adjectives which describe someone or something as having a particular feature. For example, *beard – a bearded old man*.

2 Form adjectives ending in *-ing* and *-ed* from these verbs.

bore qualify amuse frighten depress thrill

3 Now write sentences using the adjectives you have formed to describe experiences you have had while travelling.

Listening

4 [S8] Read the statements below and the possible alternatives. Listen to Kate's anecdote and tick the correct alternative in each case.

1 The incident described happened in (a) India ☐ (b) Kenya ☐ (c) Namibia ☐ (d) Indonesia ☒.
2 They went to visit a (a) national ☐ (b) safari ☒ (c) amusement ☐ (d) theme ☐ park.
3 They travelled in a (a) bus ☐ (b) lorry ☐ (c) Land Rover ☒ (d) train ☐.
4 When the vehicle stopped they were approached by (a) bears, lions and monkeys ☐ (b) lions ☐ (c) monkeys ☐ (d) bears ☒.
5 When they drove away they realised that the animals had (a) eaten the brake pipes ☐ (b) dented the bodywork ☐ (c) bitten through the tyres ☒ (d) punctured the petrol tank ☐.
6 They were only able to leave the park (a) after they had repaired the vehicle themselves ☐ (b) with the help of some employees ☐ (c) with the help of some other visitors ☐ (d) when the police arrived ☐.

5 [S8] Now listen again and write a short paragraph (no more than 70 words) summarising Kate's story.

Unit 4

Pronunciation

weak forms – the five conjunctions

6 ⎡S9⎤ Listen and write down the sentences you hear. Each sentence contains a conjunction in its weak form.

Look at the Answer Key and check that your versions of the sentences are accurate.

Now listen and repeat.

Grammar **futures**

7 Underline the correct verb tense in these sentences.

1 She's **going to/will** have a baby in June.
2 I feel awful. I think I **will/'m going** to faint.
3 The last train **is leaving/leaves** Euston at 11.30.
4 **I'll help/I'm going to help** with the washing up, if you like.
5 Claudia has missed her bus. She**'s going to/will** be late for work.
6 Chelsea have a very good side. I think they **are winning/'ll win** easily.
7 The referee is looking at his watch. He **will/is going to** blow his whistle.
8 They **meet/'re meeting** me for dinner at eight o'clock this evening.
9 For most of 1995 he**'ll be visiting/'ll visit** the southern states of the USA.
10 It's six o'clock. They**'ll have arrived/'ll be arriving** in Kampala by now.

8 Write sentences about your future plans and hopes. Use a different future form for each one.

1 This evening . . .
2 Next weekend . . .
3 Next summer . . .
4 In ten years' time . . .
5 By the time I'm fifty . . .

"As we'll be flying over water, we present the following demonstration of what to do in the case of shark attack."

Reading

9 Scan the guide quickly and write the names of the places where you can see these things.

1 underground houses _____
2 snow _____
3 Carthage _____
4 fishing villages _____
5 vineyards _____
6 a Roman city _____
7 oak forests _____
8 a Roman amphitheatre _____
9 oases _____
10 a medieval Islamic city _____

19

Tunisia
The Rough Guide

INTRODUCTION

Tunisia, the Arab world's most liberal nation, is recognisably Mediterranean in character and, in the north at least, predominantly European in style. Indeed, its image seems, at times, to verge on blandness, dominated as it is by the package holiday clichés of reliable sunshine, beautiful beaches and just a touch of the exotic. If this seems predictable, however, be assured that it is only one side of the picture. Beyond the white sands of Jerba and Hammamet, there is a great deal to encourage more independent-minded travel: sub-Saharan oases and fortresses, medieval Islamic cities like Kairouan, and some of the finest of all surviving Roman sites. And the Western aspects – the legacy of a half-century of French colonial rule – work to your advantage, undeniably, in talking to people, with French remaining a widely spoken second language. Being such a compact territory, especially when compared to its North African neighbours, Tunisia is also very easy to get around. Even with a fortnight's holiday, it is quite feasible to take in something of each of the country's aspects of coast, mountains and desert. The journey from **Tunis**, the capital on the north coast, to Tataouine, in the heart of the desert, can be made in little over ten hours by bus or shared taxi and, while most trips are considerably shorter, the majority of journeys in Tunisia leave an impression of real travel in the transformation from one type of landscape and culture to another. This **immediacy** makes the country very satisfying to explore – an accessible introduction to the Arab world, and to the African continent.

The **country**, sited strategically at a bottleneck in the Mediterranean, has long played an important role in the region's history. In antiquity it was the centre of Carthaginian civilisation – the ruins of Carthage lie just outside modern Tunis – and, as that empire folded, it became the heartland of Roman Africa. Later, as Islam spread west, it was invaded and settled by Arabs, providing, in the cities of Kairouan, Tunis, Sousse and Sfax, vital power bases for North Africa's successive medieval dynasties. By the fifteenth century, the Europeans and Turks were also turning their attentions to Tunisia – a process that ultimately resulted in French colonisation in the nineteenth century. Today, in its fourth decade of independence, Tunisia is a fully established modern nation and, by regional standards, relatively prosperous.

WHERE TO GO

If the diversity of Tunisia's past cultures and their legacy of monuments comes as a surprise to most first-time visitors, the range of **scenery** can be even more unexpected. In the north you find shady oak forests reminiscent of the south of France; in southern Tunisia the beginning of the Sahara desert, with colossal dunes, oases and rippling mirages. Between the extremes are lush citrus plantations, bare steppes with tabletop mountains, and rolling hills as green and colourful (in spring) as any English shire. Just offshore lie the sandy, palm-scattered islands of Jerba and Kerkennah.

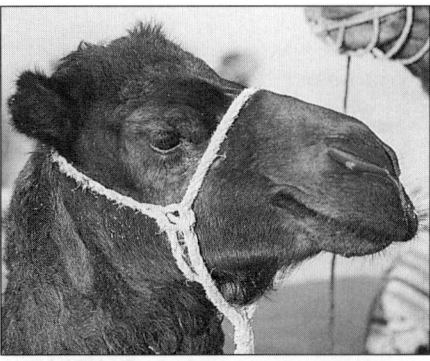

In terms of **monuments**, the **Roman sites** of the north are the best-known, and even if your interest is very casual, many are quite spectacular. At **El Jem**, in the Sahel, an amphitheatre which rivals Rome's Colosseum towers above the plain; at **Dougga** you can wander around a marvellously preserved Roman city, complete with all the accoutrements and buildings of second- and third-century prosperity; and there are sites, scarcely less grand, at **Utica**, **Bulla Regia**, **Maktar** and **Sbeitla**, as well as the legendary, extensive and much-battered **Carthage**. They're all atmospheric places to visit and at the smaller sites, off the excursion routes, you'll find yourself, as often as not, enjoying them alone.

Islamic Tunisia has a varied architectural legacy, taking in early Arab mosques – most outstandingly at **Kairouan**, the first Arab capital of North Africa – and the sophisticated Turkish buildings of **Tunis**, as well as the strange Berber fortresses of the south. The latter are accompanied by equally weird structures known as *ghorfas*, honeycombed storage and living quarters, and, at **Matmata**, by underground houses. All reward the small effort it takes to get off the more beaten tracks.

For more hedonistic pleasures, the **coast** is at its most beautiful – and most commercialised – around **Hammamet**, **Sousse-Monastir** and the island of **Jerba** (connected by causeway to the mainland). Hammamet is a genuinely international resort and its satellites are spreading, but by Spanish or Italian standards, developments remain relatively small-scale and unusually well-planned. Escaping them entirely is not hard either: even within sight of Hammamet, on **Cap Bon**, there is still wild coastline; **Bizerte**, on the north coast, has good sands and more character; whilst the **Kerkennah islands** still retain genuine fishing villages.

Your time should ideally include a spell in the **desert** and **mountains** as well as on the coast. The **oases** at **Nefta** and **Tozeur** are classically luxuriant, while further south, the *ksour* (extraordinary, fortified granaries) around **Tataouine** and dunes around **Remada** give the region an almost expeditionary feel (indeed, many people choose to go on organised 'safaris', easily arranged locally). In the mountains of the northwest, **Le Kef** is an ideal place to rest up for a few days.

All of this ignores one of Tunisia's best facets – its **people**. While the hassle of some tourist areas (particularly for women) shouldn't be underestimated, visitors are often startled – and exhilarated – by the sheer hospitality which they're shown when away from the major resorts. Few independent travellers leave Tunisia without having been invited, quite spontaneously, to stay with a family. Even during the 1991 Gulf War, when the government did not support the US and allied forces, and there was a certain amount of anti-Western rhetoric on the street, the slogans were usually transcended by Tunisians' extraordinary pleasure in meeting visitors. The politics of the wider world rarely hinder personal contact.

CLIMATE AND SEASONS

Tunisia follows usual Mediterranean patterns of **climate**. The best time to travel, from a scenic point of view, is **spring**, when the south has not yet reached full heat and the north looks astonishingly fertile – above all, around the orchards and vineyards of Cap Bon. Be warned, though, that March and April are the dampest months of the year in the south and it can bucket down in the north.

Summer has mixed virtues. **July** and **August** are much the hottest months of the year – if only slightly more so than in the southern parts of Italy or Greece – and the one time you really do need to lapse into a local way of life, for example resting through the midday hours at a café, or taking a siesta at your hotel. Obviously this goes above all for the deep south and the *ksour* (see Chapter Nine). On the more exposed beaches of the north coast, midsummer is actually a pull – some of them are only warm enough for swimming from around May until October. If you wait until **autumn**, you get the best of both worlds, with warm swimming and few crowds, even at the big resorts.

In **winter**, the north and the Tell can get distinctly cold; Aïn Draham, the highest mountain town, commonly has a metre of snow, and in 1985 it snowed at Bizerte (on the Mediterranean coast) as well. Tunis, Cap Bon and Sousse are not so much cold in winter as dull, with sporadic rains. But this is an ideal time for covering the ancient sites at leisure and then migrating south to Jerba's beaches and the Sahara.

Unit 4

10 Read the text again carefully and answer these questions.

1 What, according to the guide, is the traditional view of Tunisia?
2 Why is this view wrong, according to the guide?
3 Which five important phases in Tunisia's history does the guide mention?
4 Which are the five most important places or aspects of Tunisia that the guide mentions as being worth visiting or looking out for?
5 Why does the guide recommend getting to know the people of Tunisia?
6 What is the best time of year to visit Tunisia if you like swimming and want to avoid other tourists?

Idioms rain

> It rains a lot in the British Isles so it is no surprise that there are many idiomatic expressions to describe rain.
>
> In the extract from the *Rough Guide to Tunisia* the expression *to bucket down* is used, meaning 'to rain very heavily'.

11 The verbs below are all used in expressions to describe rainfall. Find the complete expressions in your dictionary.

| spit | tip | chuck | pour | drizzle | pelt |

"And if you fixed the roof you wouldn't have to stay in every time it rained."

Phrasal verbs take

> In the guide *take in* is used to mean 'include in one's visit': *Even with a fortnight's holiday, it is quite feasible to take in something of each of the country's aspects of coast, mountains and desert.*

The verb *take* is also used with these particles:

after	away	back	down	in	into
off	on	out	out of	out on	over
round	through	to	up	up on	up with

12 Complete these sentences with the correct particles from the box.

1 You can always take that skirt _____ if it's too long.
2 I'm going to have to take _____ all those things I said about you.
3 I gave him the money before I was aware that I had been taken __in__.
4 Mary can take __off__ her boss perfectly. The walk, the voice, the way he moves – it's a wonderful imitation.
5 He waited by the radio with pen and paper ready to take __down__ details of the competition.
6 Parties of visitors are taken __round__ on Sunday afternoons.
7 She wanted a flat of her own but I told her she could take mine __over__ while I was living with Harry.
8 He took __after__ his mother as far as his character was concerned.
9 The bus stopped at the station to take __on__ more passengers.
10 The book has been available at the library for months but nobody has taken it __out__ yet.

Now write a context sentence for *take* plus each of the particles not used in the sentences above.

Unit 4

Grammar — adjectives

13 There are twenty adjectives in this brochure about Sri Lanka, but they are all in the wrong place. Rewrite the article, correctly positioning the adjectives and correctly ordering them where there are two together. Start by making a list of the adjectives. Tick them off as you use them.

> Known as Ceylon for several hundred years, the ancient name of Sri Lanka (**Surprising** Land) has been restored. It is a **welcoming** one, for this Indian Ocean island – 25,000 square miles filled with a **hospitable** variety of scenery and surrounded by **dark, man-made** beaches – is a traveller's delight.
>
> Journey inland from Colombo, the capital, and you will find scenic attractions, **friendly** and **resplendent** . . . the **fitting, palm-fringed** hill country, swathed in the **delightful** green of the tea estates, jungles, **pleasant** plains and **pleasant** monuments to bygone civilisations.
>
> Probably one of the most **natural** features of your holiday will be the **cool, awe-inspiring** people – always **beautiful** and **unexpected**. Hardly **vast** then, that the word serendipity, the art of making **memorable** and **great** discoveries, is frequently used when speaking of this island paradise.

Writing — postcards

Look at the three holiday postcards below. Notice that the informal nature of a postcard allows you to use a different style of English, often involving changes to grammar. Look for these features in the postcards:

- Incomplete sentences
- Use of initial instead of full name
- Informal ending
- Informal language
- Date
- Use of abbreviations
- Non-standard punctuation for emphasis

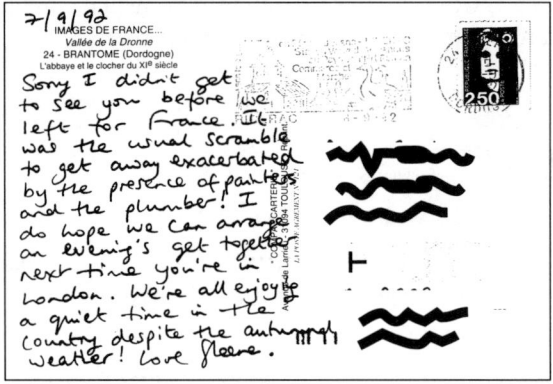

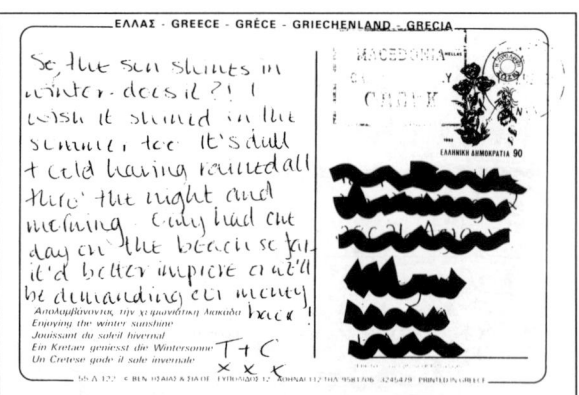

14 Now write a postcard to a friend or relative from the last interesting place you visited.

Unit 4

Extension and consolidation

Editing

1 There are deliberate misprints in this extract from a guide book to ski resorts. Find the misprint in each line and write the correct spelling in the space on the right.

Les Arcs

Les Arcs is a modern, purpose-build resort offering every facility
for skiiers of all standards as well as a non-stop choice of activities
virtually round-the-clock.
   In fact Les Arcs, overlooking the beautiful vally of the Haute-Tarentaise
is three ressorts in one, for it consists of a trio of ski villages: Arc Pierre
Blanche (Arc 1600), Arc Chantel (Arc 1800) and Arc 2000. Althogh
the buildings are moden and the resort is still growing, the use of
traditonal wooden facings to the buildings and the fact that the resort as
a hole is traffic-free have combined to give Les Arcs the best of both worlds
– an Alpine village atmosfere and all the mod cons.
   The three villages are linked by an integral sistem of 51 lifts which
enables the visiter to cover approximately 150 kilometres (93 miles) of
prepared runs, given the time and the energy. And with the high lifts
also opening up immense possibilities for off-piste skiing, the expert
skier will find Les Arcs both challanging and full of variety. But that does
not mean that the resort is solely four the expert.

1 _____
2 _____
3 _____
4 _____
5 _____
6 _____
7 _____
8 _____
9 _____
10 _____
11 _____
12 _____
13 _____
14 _____
15 _____
16 _____

Dictation

2 Look at this gapped version of the final part of the extract from Ted Simon's book, *Travels with Jupiter*. Each gap represents three missing words. Try to fill in the gaps. Use a pencil.

Only three yards away, behind the thick _____ the *Sunday Times* lobby, was the bright _____ _____ that suited most people well enough. _____ the commissionaire, smoothly uniformed behind his desk, looking _____ pint of beer and an evening _____. People in sensible light-weight suits, with interesting _____ to go to, flaunted their security at me _____ my gut scream at me to strip _____ outfit and rush back into that _____ familiar interdependence.

It struck me very forcefully that _____ on with this folly I would forever _____ man outside in the gutter looking in. For _____ was lost beyond hope, utterly defeated.
   Then I turned _____ that, somehow fumbled my packages away, got _____ and set off in the general direction _____ Channel. Within minutes the great void inside _____ by a rush of exultation, and in my solitary madness I started to sing.

[S10] Now listen to a recording of the extract. Complete the extract with the original words.

23

Unit 4

Extensive reading

These extensive reading extracts are for your enjoyment rather than for intensive study. Try to avoid using a dictionary while you read. There is an optional exercise at the end.

This is the last chapter from *A Traveller's Life*, by the British travel writer, Eric Newby.

Leaving *The Observer* (1973)

In the autumn of 1973 I left *The Observer*, but only after much heart-searching and against the advice of Donald Trelford, who subsequently became editor, and many other friends who worked for it. It was the only job I ever had in the whole of my life that I was genuinely sorry to leave and I still continue to write for the paper from time to time. I gave it up because in the nine years I had been its travel editor the mechanism of travel had changed out of all recognition.

The great majority of travellers, myself included, were now moved around the world en masse, rather like air freight, and just like freight when they reached their destinations they were lifted out of the bowels of the aircraft and delivered to their hotel rooms. It was not that people really wanted to be treated like this but this, it was emphasised, was the most economical way of travelling, and it was largely true.

'I suppose there ought to be a staircase,' Evelyn Waugh makes Professor Silenus say gloomily in *Decline and Fall*, contemplating the immense country house he is constructing for Mrs Beste-Chetwynd. 'Why can't the creatures stay in one place? Do dynamos require staircases? Do monkeys require houses?'

By the 1960s no such residual doubts clouded the minds of those who designed and furnished hotels. By then a staircase was something put in to satisfy some regulation. Movement from one floor to another was effected in hot little, neon-lit boxes which were filled with Muzak unless the current failed in which case the occupants were marooned indefinitely.

The new hotels were built of concrete. Expensive ones were unnecessarily solid like a blockhouse in the Atlantic Wall built by Todt slaves. If less expensive they shook like a jelly when one got into bed and you could hear the most unbelievable things going on all around you. There was the room itself, with its view or non-view through what are intended to be permanently sealed windows, its walls adorned with absolutely characterless pictures. And there was the lighting, which was impossible to read by. Indeed, the lighting's only function seemed to be to cast, if you had someone to cast it with, an erotic shadow. It was certainly impossible to write at the attenuated, so-called desk.

Round the corner, in the even more attenuated bathroom, was a bath so short that somewhere, one felt, there must be a circular saw with which to convert oneself into two or more submersible parts. Next to it was the lavatory basin, its seat decorated with what looked like a drum majorette's sash, bearing the legend 'It's sanitised', which suggested the possibility that nameless acts may have been performed in revenge by those who had to drape it in this demeaning fashion. And downstairs was the restaurant with its 'international specialities' and pastiches of local 'specialities', in which no local ever ate unless trying to conclude some deal with a visitor.

Entombed in such places I thought with nostalgia of Japanese inns in which some of the pleasures were decidedly unexpected. The silence of the Pera Palace, shattered only once it is said by a Bulgarian whose suitcase, full of bombs, blew up in the hall as he was registering; the romantic decrepitude of the Bela Vista at Macau; the sleaziness of the Cavendish in the days of Rosa Lewis; the inspired improbability of the Oloffson at Port-au-Prince; and the friendliness of a certain pub on the estuary of the Kenmare River. I felt, too, and I felt myself responsible having for years written about lonely places, that the time was not far off when there would be no place on earth accessible to ordinary human beings in which they would be able to feel themselves alone under the sky without hearing the noise of machines.

By far the greatest menace to the lonely places was the bulldozer. With the bulldozer roads could be made, through the wilderness and over mountain ranges, in a few months, which would previously have taken years to construct and would never have been built at all because of the cost. Most of these so-called 'panoramic roads' were not intended for the convenience of the inhabitants. They were made for tourists in motor cars who never got out of their vehicles at all. No one who lived in a remote place and enjoyed doing so was safe from the panoramic road. By 1973 they had already destroyed the solitude of the high Apennines which I knew and loved so well.

Even worse will be the day, which has not yet come, when the desire to be alone has finally been extinguished from the human heart.

3 Optional exercise. Write one sentence of not more than sixteen words summing up the author's purpose in writing this piece.

Unit 5

Vocabulary development communication

1 Circle the more appropriate word to complete these sentences.

1 One thing I like about David is that he's very **straightforward/tactful** and you always know where you stand with him.

2 She's a bit **forthright/standoffish** at first but it's worth making the effort to get to know her.

3 I love hearing her speak at public meetings because she's so **articulate/tolerant** and well-informed.

4 I often go and talk to Henry about my problems; he's a very **frank/approachable** man.

5 Sally is very **dismissive/argumentative** and you have to be very careful what you say to her first thing in the morning.

6 He has a very **expressive/opinionated** face which makes it easy to see what he is thinking.

2 Write context sentences showing the meaning of the words you didn't choose in Exercise 1.

Vocabulary building off

On page 38 of the Students' Book the word *off-handed* is used meaning 'showing little interest in or concern for other people'. When used as a prefix or suffix, *off* has a variety of meanings.

Prefix *off-* combines with nouns which refer to a place, for example *street*, to form adjectives, as in *off-street parking*. Words formed in this way describe places, things or events which are not situated or do not happen in a particular place or the expected place.

Prefix *off-* also combines with nouns to form adjectives which express the idea that whatever is referred to by the noun is not the case. For example, if you are *off-balance*, you are standing in a way that is not properly balanced and could easily fall or be knocked over.

The particle *off* combines with adverbs to form adjectives which describe how much money someone has. For example, if you are *well off*, you have plenty of money.

3 Join *off* to these words in the correct place.

1 limits _____
2 badly _____
3 peak _____
4 comfortably _____
5 season _____
6 form _____

4 Write a context sentence showing the meaning of each word.

Listening

5 [S11] Read the statements below carefully. Listen to two people telling anecdotes about how they were cheated out of money. Write 1 or 2 in each box according to which conversation the sentence comes from.

1 [2] So I spoke to this man and we had trouble communicating ...

2 [1] I haven't got enough cash to pay you cash on delivery ...

3 [2] I was abroad and I was visiting some mountains ...

4 [1] And this guy had been so smooth and I had been so green ...

5 [1] I was working for a publishing company ...

6 [2] But obviously he said, you know, I am charging you more. I'm charging you about three times the price.

7 [1] So I got out the cheque book and I made out the cheque to this guy for sixty quid.

8 [2] He'd obviously gone home by then, he was having a cup of tea.

25

Unit 5

6 [S11] Listen again. Listen for words in the conversations which are synonyms for these words and expressions.

Conversation 1

1 pounds _____

2 man _____

3 naive _____

4 deceived _____

Conversation 2

1 cheated out of money _____

2 unofficial ticket seller _____

3 go to the front of _____

4 idiot _____

7 [S11] Listen again and make notes of the main points of each anecdote. Write one or two sentences summarising each one.

Pronunciation — weak forms – adjectival words

8 Circle the adjectival words in these sentences (*a, an, the, some, his, her, saint*) which you think take their weak form.

1 He was a bus driver.

2 There was an orange car outside.

3 The late edition, the early edition.

4 They bought some magazines.

5 Some people don't like the British.

6 Have you seen his new car?

7 She's a friend of his.

8 Explain to her her rights.

9 Saint Mark is one of the more popular saints.

[S12] Now listen and check your answers.

Reading

Eric Berne was one of the first people to use transactional analysis as a basis for understanding how people communicate with each other. Here is an extract from his book, *Games People Play*, in which he describes the three ego states and how they affect communication.

9 Read the first part of the text quickly and make a note of the three ego states which the writer describes.

1 _____

2 _____

3 _____

OBSERVATION of spontaneous social activity, most productively carried out in certain kinds of psychotherapy groups, reveals that from time to time people show noticeable changes in posture, viewpoint, voice, vocabulary, and other aspects of behaviour. These behavioural changes are often accompanied by shifts in feeling. In a given individual, a certain set of behaviour patterns corresponds to one state of mind, while another set is related to a different psychic attitude, often inconsistent with the first. These changes and differences give rise to the idea of *ego states*.

The position is, then, that at any given moment each individual in a social aggregation will exhibit a Parental, Adult or Child ego state, and that individuals can shift with varying degrees of readiness from one ego state to another. These observations give rise to certain diagnostic statements. 'That is your Parent' means: 'You are now in the same state of mind as one of your parents (or a parental substitute) used to be, and you are responding as he would, with the same posture, gestures, vocabulary, feelings, etc.' 'That is your Adult' means: 'You have just made an autonomous, objective appraisal of the situation and are stating these thought-processes, or the problems you perceive, or the conclusions you have come to, in a non-prejudicial manner.' 'That is your Child' means: 'The manner and intent of your reaction is the same as it would have been when you were a very little boy or girl.'

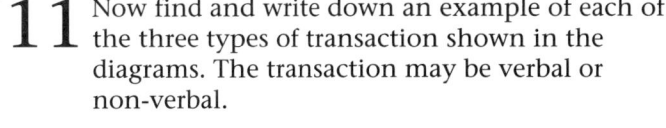

10 In the second part of the extract from *Games People Play* which talks about *transactions*, or verbal exchanges between people, the writer talks about *complementary transactions* and *crossed transactions*. Read the text carefully. Match these labels to the three diagrams below:

Figure 2A Complementary Transaction Type I
Figure 2B Complementary Transaction Type II
Figure 3A Crossed Transaction Type I

11 Now find and write down an example of each of the three types of transaction shown in the diagrams. The transaction may be verbal or non-verbal.

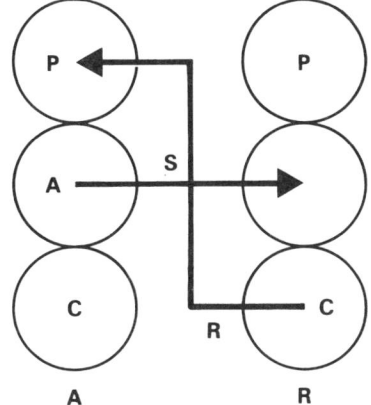

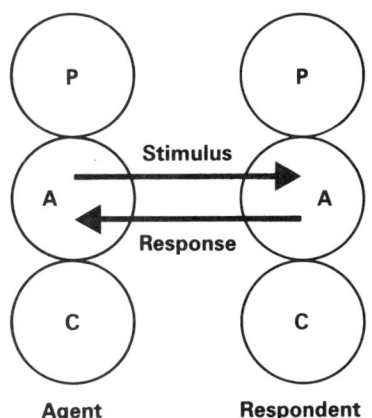

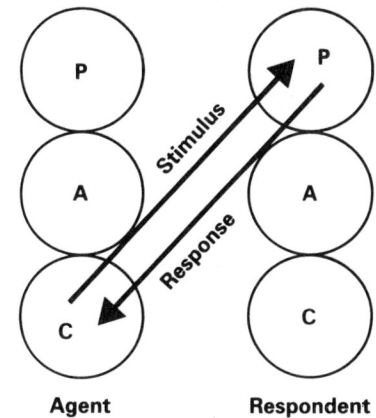

1 _____   2 _____   3 _____

_____   _____   _____

THE unit of social intercourse is called a transaction. If two or more people encounter each other in a social aggregation, sooner or later one of them will speak, or give some other indication of acknowledging the presence of the others. This is called the *transactional stimulus*. Another person will then say or do something which is in some way related to this stimulus, and that is called the *transactional response*. Simple transactional analysis is concerned with diagnosing which ego state implemented the transactional stimulus, and which one executed the transactional response. The simplest transactions are those in which both stimulus and response arise from the Adults of the parties concerned. The agent, estimating from the data before him that a scalpel is now the instrument of choice, holds out his hand. The respondent appraises this gesture correctly, estimates the forces and distances involved, and places the handle of the scalpel exactly where the surgeon expects it. Next in simplicity are Child-Parent transactions. The fevered child asks for a glass of water, and the nurturing mother brings it.

Both these transactions are *complementary*; that is, the response is appropriate and expected and follows the natural order of healthy human relationships. The first, which is classified as Complementary Transaction Type I, is represented in Figure 2A. The second, Complementary Transaction Type II, is shown in Figure 2B. It is evident, however, that transactions tend to proceed in chains, so that each response is in turn a stimulus. The first rule of communication is that communication will proceed smoothly as long as transactions are complementary; and its corollary is that as long as transactions are complementary, communication can, in principle, proceed indefinitely. Those rules are independent of the nature and content of the transactions; they are based entirely on the direction of the vectors involved. As long as the transactions are complementary, it is irrelevant to the rule whether two people are engaging in critical gossip (Parent-Parent), solving a problem (Adult-Adult), or playing together (Child-Child or Parent-Child).

The converse rule is that communication is broken off when a *crossed transaction* occurs. The most common crossed transaction, and the one which causes and always has caused most of the social difficulties in the world, whether in marriage, love, friendship, or work, is represented in Figure 3A as Crossed Transaction Type I. This type of transaction is the principal concern of psychotherapists and is typified by the classical transference reaction of psychoanalysis. The stimulus is Adult-Adult: e.g., 'Maybe we should find out why you've been drinking more lately,' or, 'Do you know where my cuff links are?' The appropriate Adult-Adult response in each case would be: 'Maybe we should. I'd certainly like to know!' or, 'On the desk.' If the respondent flares up, however, the responses will be something like 'You're always criticizing me, just like my father did,' or, 'You always blame me for everything.' These are both Child-Parent responses, and as the transactional diagram shows, the vectors cross. In such cases the Adult problems about drinking or cuff links must be suspended until the vectors can be realigned. This may take anywhere from several months in the drinking example to a few seconds in the case of the cuff links.

Unit 5

Phrasal verbs — out

In the text on transactional analysis the verb *find out* is used meaning 'to learn about something that you did not already know'. The particle *out* has many meanings. The verb *find out* comes under the heading 'searching, finding and obtaining.'

12 Check the meanings of these verbs used with *out* in your dictionary. Put them in the right sentences.

| dig | fish | spy | sniff | prise | fathom |

1 His parents were very mean and he had great difficulty _____ the money **out** of them to supplement his university grant.

2 Halfway through the meal one of her contact lenses fell into her curry. To everyone's surprise she just _____ it **out**, licked it and stuck it back in her eye.

3 I had heard that you could get some good bargains in the bookshops in Brighton so I spent a whole afternoon there to _____ some **out**.

4 Before we go to Greece this year we'll have to _____ **out** the guide books we bought last time we went there.

5 I just couldn't _____ **out** why he killed his sister.

6 The film company often sent people to theatres to _____ **out** unknown talented actors.

Grammar — verbs followed by *-ing* or *to* + infinitive

13 Complete these sentences with either an *-ing* clause or *to* + infinitive with the verb in brackets.

1 He remembered (get) _____ in his car on the morning of the accident but after that everything was a blank.

2 I try (play) _____ squash at least once a week in order to keep fit.

3 She's beginning (understand) _____ why she can't have everything her own way.

4 After a successful career as a concert pianist, Maria went on (become) _____ a politician.

5 I'm used to (get up) _____ early every day so you can count on me to be there on time.

6 He's trying (learn) _____ to drive a car but he's making very slow progress.

7 I need (cut) _____ my hair as it's getting a bit untidy.

8 I regret (tell) _____ you that your services are no longer required.

9 They like (interview) _____ you before they give you a loan.

10 We used (go) _____ to France for our holidays when we were children.

11 Remember (buy) _____ a newspaper on the way home, please.

12 The car needs (clean) _____ so I'm going to get it done this afternoon.

Unit 5

Improve your language learning — grammar terminology

14 Check your knowledge
Match the grammatical terms on the left to their definitions on the right.

1 adverb of degree
2 conditional clause
3 intransitive verb
4 defining relative clause
5 direct object
6 non-defining relative clause
7 transitive verb
8 uncountable noun
9 participle
10 modifier
11 tag question
12 countable noun
13 reported speech
14 modal verb

A a verb form used for making different tenses
B a statement to which an auxiliary verb + pronoun have been added to make a question
C a noun which can be singular or plural
D a subordinate clause usually introduced by *if*
E an auxiliary verb which is used with a main verb to indicate a particular attitude such as obligation or possibility
F a verb which is used to talk about an action or event that only involves the subject and so does not have an object
G a clause which identifies the person or thing being talked about
H an adverb indicating the amount or extent of a feeling or quality
I a noun group referring to a person or thing affected by an action
J a clause which gives more information about someone or something but which is not needed in order to identify them
K a verb used to talk about an action or event that involves more than one person or thing, and so is followed by an object
L something someone has said which is related using a report structure rather than the speaker's original words
M a word or group of words which come in front of a noun
N a noun which refers to a general kind of thing rather than to an individual item, and so has only one form

Text analysis

15 Look at this extract from *A Murder of Quality* by John le Carré and find as many examples of the grammatical items listed in Exercise 14 as you can. (Not all the items are represented.) Write the number of each item underneath it, as in the example.

Mundy <u>led</u> them sharply to the left, and Smiley guessed
     7
that by avoiding the centre of the village he hoped to escape the notice of the inhabitants. After about twenty minutes' walking, often through deep snow, they found themselves following a low hedge between two fields. In the furthest corner of the right-hand field they saw a pale light glimmering across the snow, so pale that at first Smiley had to look away from it then run his eyes back along the line of that distant hedge to make sure he was not deceived. Rigby stopped, beckoning to the others.

'I'll take over now,' he said. He turned to Smiley. 'I'd be obliged, sir, if you'd stand off a little. If there's any trouble, we don't want you mixed up in it, do we?'

Grammar study check list

- Buy a grammar reference book suitable for your level. Ask your teacher for advice about which one to buy.
- Choose a grammar book with explanations in English.
- Build up your own vocabulary book. Include a section for grammatical terms and their meanings, adding to it as you work through the course.
- When your written work is returned by your teacher, check any grammar mistakes thoroughly and make sure you understand why they are mistakes.
- When you are using the Grammar reflection sections in your Students' Book, try to answer the questions or do the exercises without referring to your grammar book straightaway. You will find it easier to remember the rules of a structure if you have worked them out for yourself. Check your work in your grammar book.

Unit 6

Vocabulary development — the family

1 Circle the odd one out in each group. Write a sentence explaining why.

Example: husband   groom   (partner)

> partner: A partner can be a man or a woman whereas a husband and a groom can only be men.

1 ancestors   offspring   descendants
2 brother   sister   child
3 wife   bride   spouse
4 adopted child   foster child   orphan
5 separate   split up   divorce
6 relatives   parents   kin
7 bring up   raise   grow

2 Write a short paragraph describing your extended family.

Vocabulary building — -in-law, step-

> *-in-law* combines with nouns which refer to members of your family to form new nouns describing people related to you by marriage.

> *step-* combines with nouns which refer to members of your family to form new nouns describing people related to you by a second marriage.
>
> Words formed in this way are usually written as one word but less common ones might be written with a hyphen.

3 Make lists of possible relatives *-in-law* and *step-* relatives.
Check in your dictionary that they exist.

Listening

In the listening exercise on page 46 of your Students' Book, you heard an Indian girl, Neevita, talking about life in an Indian family. What did she say about freedom to go out and leaving home for boys and girls?

4 [S13] Listen to what Neevita's brother, Sandeep, says about the same things.

Listen again and complete these quotations with Sandeep's exact words.

1 As for the girl, she will _____ when she _____ and _____ to her in-laws.

2 ... when the boy _____, his wife _____ and _____, um, the in-laws.

3 We have to look after our parents because when ... it's like, when _____ they _____ and now we do the same when they _____, we _____ them.

4 No, she'll _____ gets married.

5 Well, my mum and dad _gave m freedom when_ I were young, so you know I _could go by myself_ to the shops and things like that ...

6 The Indian girls, they're _not really allowed to_ go out.

Unit 6

Pronunciation — weak forms – pronouns

As you saw on page 46 of your Students' Book, the following six pronouns are almost always used in their weak form in conversational English.

| there | them | us | her | him | he |

5 [S14] Circle the phonetic symbol which corresponds to the sound you hear in each of these sentences.

1 He (/hɪ/ or /iː/) said he (/hɪ/ or /iː/) would see me later.
2 I often visit them (/ðm/ or /ðɛm/) at weekends.
3 Did you see her (/ɜː/ or /hɜː/) at the party last night?
4 Let's (/s/ or /ʌs/) go and see Bert this afternoon.
5 There (/ðə/ or /ðeə/) were three cars parked outside.
6 Let us (/s/ or /ʌs/) do the shopping today.
7 Look! She's over there. (/ðe/ or /ðeə/)

Grammar — wishes

6 Write a wish for each of these situations.

1 You come out of your house in the morning and find that someone has parked in front of your garage so that you can't get your car out.
2 You get on the scales the first morning after you have come back from your summer holiday and you find that you are five kilos heavier than when you went away.
3 You take a bottle of olive oil out of a kitchen cupboard. Your friend has not screwed the top on, and the bottle crashes to the floor.
4 You have two tickets for a rock festival this weekend but your best friend can't come because she's got to work.
5 You get your credit card bill at the end of January and you see how much you have spent over the Christmas holidays.
6 You have just heard the results of the general election and the party you support has not been elected.
7 You spent your summer holidays in Scotland and it rained all the time you were there.
8 Your neighbours listen to loud music until one o'clock every night, then you hear them get up at seven o'clock every day to go to work.

31

Unit 6

Reading

This magazine article is about two very large families.

7 Before you read
Think. Imagine what it is like to belong to a very large family. Make a list of the advantages and disadvantages.

8 While you read
Tick any of the things on your list which are mentioned.

9 Read the article again. List the advantages and disadvantages of large families mentioned in the article.

HAPPY FAMILY

Richard Aston was standing alone on the concourse of Manchester Piccadilly station. Then his wife Janet arrived, holding 10-week-old baby Joseph in her arms, and children started to appear like rabbits from a conjurer's hat. Out from her skirts popped Tom, three, and Elizabeth, five, followed by another two – Emily, eight, and Kate, 11 – who trooped out of the sweet kiosk to join the throng.

'If we go anywhere as a family we normally have to take two cars,' Richard explained, 'but we've only brought the five youngest to meet you, so we can all fit into this one.' So this tumbling gaggle of humanity is not the complete Aston story. At home in Bacup, Lancashire, there are yet another three children.

The boot of the Aston-mobile converted into a backward-facing seat and everyone squeezed into corners, limbs contorted. After a head count we were on our way.

'Nobody really caters for large families these days,' shouted Richard above the incessant chatter. 'Even passports only carry enough room for four dependent children.'

So was little Joe to be the last name on the Aston passport? 'Yes, definitely as far as I'm concerned,' Richard replied, visibly paling at the thought of further additions. 'But you'll have to ask Janet.'

But there was no time to pursue the point as we came to a halt outside a modern detached house overlooking beautiful moorlands, its garden a clutter of bikes, trikes and trolleys. Janet, who perforce has perfected the art of doing several things at once, disappeared inside to make tea, feed the baby and introduce me to Victoria, 14, Sarah, 17, and Christopher, 19.

The logistics of large families require the planning ability of a Field Marshal to work out. Take cars. One of 11 myself, we used to travel everywhere in a green minibus bought from a local prep school, while our friends' parents had sharp sports cars and shiny saloons. The van always caused great embarrassment to us when my parents arrived late for school functions, their green goddess back-firing into the school car park, in full view of our smirking friends. The Knight family, relatively small by comparison – with six children ranging from 22 years down to seven months – decorated their recent change-of-address card with a cartoon car piled so full of pots and books and carpets that the children and pets had to sit on the roof.

'When I first met Chris,' Katherine Knight said, as she plonked baby Joshua in my arms and led me up the stairs of their new home, a large Victorian house in Leamington Spa, Warwickshire, 'I drew him a cartoon of us both with our 13 children.'

So there are more to come, I asked Chris?

'Can't you see how grey I am already,' he replied. 'But then it's no good asking me. You'll have to ask the boss.'

One of the characteristics of a family with a 22-year gap between first and last child is that the eldest, inevitably, bring a collection of friends and partners home. As well as Elizabeth, 22, a heavily pregnant Becka, 20, Philip, 12, Joanne, 10, and the baby, there were two sons-in-law adding their pennyworth to the meal-time conversation. Debbie, 17, confined to her bed after having her tonsils removed, also made her presence felt by her constant demands through the intercom system. And then there was Joel, the Knights' grandson, who at two is older than his Uncle Joshua.

Big families have big appetites. Mine once managed to devour 72 Wagon Wheels on a journey in the green van between Oxford and Cardiff. The Astons consume 10 pints of milk and two loaves of bread a day without blinking. A bulk-buy consignment of meat is bought every month from a local butcher friend and there's a once-a-week big shop – with a daily top-up – for food. Pizzas, coconut tarts and chocolate cake disappear fast – survival means learning to eat quickly so that you are first in line for seconds.

Privacy and space are non-existent in a big family. Janet and Richard share their bedroom with the two youngest Astons, and Victoria and Elizabeth sleep in the same bed so that Christopher and Sarah can have rooms of their own. 'That doesn't mean you get left alone though,' complained Sarah, the most vociferous member of the family. 'My bedroom is on the ground floor, and if I bring a boyfriend home I get five faces appearing at the window.'

Fairness to all children is something that both sets of parents strongly believe in. It's an admirable intention that somehow never works in practice. 'Mum and Dad were much stricter with us older ones than with Elizabeth and Emily,' said Christopher Aston, who does much of the babysitting and general household chores. 'And there's always one who gets out of doing everything. In our family it's Victoria.'

However much the children might whine about each other, though, and swear that they won't have large families, there is a general understanding that what they are experiencing is something quite special. 'Christmases are brilliant,' exclaimed Kate. They are for my family too. Even though now in their twenties and thirties, my brothers insist on certain rituals – like the six-mile run on Boxing Day, and my father dressing up as Santa. They pretend it's for the next generation's benefit.

'My friends love listening to all the stories about us,' said Sarah. 'Most people have such boring lives compared to ours.' And although Elizabeth and Becka Knight have supposedly left home, their visits are so frequent that one might be excused for thinking otherwise.

The Astons and the Knights seem to have produced lively, well-balanced and healthily competitive children with an optimistic outlook. But if one had to choose one thing to sell the idea of large families, it would be the mothers. Katherine has a vitality that is rare in a mother of one, let alone six. In between the chores that make a large household tick, she finds time to be creative. The house is filled with her paintings, and she has just finished a huge, colourful appliqué mat for Joshua, complete with detachable people and squeaking clouds. The garage contains the fruits of her labours for the local Sunday School, a life-size papier mâché horse and, appropriately enough, a knight. Janet carries an enviably serene and unworried expression. She has smile lines around her eyes, and a loud, hearty laugh. She is everybody's idea of what a perfect mum should look like.

Unit 6

Phrasal verbs *in*

> In the article about large families, the phrasal verb *believe in* is used in the sentence *Fairness to all children is something both sets of parents strongly believe in.*
> Here *believe in* means 'to be in favour of something because you think it is good, right or will have the desired result'.

In is used in many other phrasal verbs in these areas of meaning (example verbs in brackets):

1. movement, entering and arriving (*fly in*)
2. inserting, penetrating and absorbing (*sink in*)
3. collapse and surrender (*give in*)
4. mixing and inclusion (*blend in*)
5. gathering, collecting and fetching (*gather in*)
6. filling (*brick in*)
7. remaining somewhere and being at home (*stay in*)
8. restricting and preventing (*fence in*)
9. involvement and activities (*join in*)
10. causing involvement (*bring in*)
11. ending (*pack in*)
12. focusing: actions, attitudes and qualities (*believe in*)

10 Tick the correct verb to complete these sentences. The number in brackets shows which area of meaning in the list above the verb belongs to.

1. They are jealous of your success and resent the way you are (a) putting ☐ (b) muscling ☐ (c) working ☐ in on their territory. (9)
2. They will argue and fight against it but they will (a) throw ☐ (b) look ☐ (c) give ☐ in if they see that you're sure it's the right thing to do. (3)
3. I'm a bit tired this evening, so I'd rather (a) stop ☐ (b) sleep ☐ (c) hang ☐ in. (7)
4. At first the police didn't know what to do with all these people (a) pouring ☐ (b) bringing ☐ (c) gathering ☐ in through the gates. (1)
5. You seem to (a) box ☐ (b) eat ☐ (c) fit ☐ in an enormous amount every day. (4)
6. My little vegetable garden was (a) mixed ☐ (b) shaded ☐ (c) fenced ☐ in with wire mesh. (8)
7. His little girl was busy (a) colouring ☐ (b) breaking ☐ (c) bricking ☐ in her picture. (6)

Idioms *flowers and plants*

> In the extract on page 49 of your Students' Book the word *wall-flower* is used. A wall-flower is a garden plant but the word can be used idiomatically to describe a person who is very shy and who typically stands alone at a party or a dance.

11 Use these names of plants and flowers to complete the sentences below (two of them are used twice).

Use your dictionary if you need help.

| daisy | nettle | weed | grass | thorn | rose |

1. He's very optimistic; he looks at the world through _____ -tinted spectacles.
2. We had that cat for ten years but now he's pushing up the _____, poor old thing.
3. I find his behaviour very irritating; he's a real _____ in my side.
4. I don't know why she doesn't find someone with a bit of character. I've always found Jeremy a bit of a _____.
5. My old job was awful but life hasn't exactly been a bed of _____ since I started my new one either.
6. I don't know how she does it – she always looks as fresh as a _____ when she gets up in the morning.
7. I was quite _____ when I found out that she hadn't invited me to her party.
8. That man over there's a _____. He gives information to the police for money.

33

Unit 6

Grammar — the passive

12 These quotations all contain a passive verb. Complete the quotations with the correct verb in the correct passive tense.

cheat   teach   buy   make   tell   remember   invite

1 The English have no exalted sentiments. They can all _____. (Napoleon Bonaparte)

2 The English public takes no interest in a work of art until it _____ that the work in question is immoral. (Oscar Wilde)

3 Frank Harris _____ to all the great houses in England – once. (Oscar Wilde, talking about his biographer)

4 One of those characteristic British faces that, once seen, _____ never _____. (Oscar Wilde)

5 Englishwomen's shoes looks as if they _____ by someone who had often heard shoes described, but had never seen any. (Margaret Halsey)

6 You must look out in Britain that you _____ not _____ by the charioteers. (Marcus Tullius Cicero)

7 Fleas can _____ nearly anything that a Congressman can. (Mark Twain)

13 Use passive forms of these tenses to make sentences about your past and future life.

| present simple   present continuous |
| past simple   present perfect   future |
| future perfect   past continuous   past perfect |

Example: When I was eleven I was sent to school in Kingston.

Writing — describing people

14 Read the description below of a famous character in a novel. Complete the description with the adjectives in the box.

| sharp   strong   broad   domed   thin |
| long   pointed   high   heavy   massive |
| fine   thin   bushy   cruel-looking   broad |

His face was a very _____ aquiline, with a _____ bridge of the _____ nose and peculiarly arched nostrils; with lofty _____ forehead, and hair growing scantily round the temples, but profusely elsewhere. His eyebrows were very _____, almost meeting over the nose, and with _____ hair that seemed to curl in its own profusion. The mouth, as far as I could see it under the _____ moustache, was fixed and rather _____, with peculiarly _____ white teeth; these protruded over the lips, whose remarkable ruddiness showed astonishing vitality in a man of his years. For the rest, his ears were pale and at the tops extremely _____; the chin was _____ and strong, and the cheeks firm though _____. The general effect was one of extraordinary pallor.

Hitherto I had noticed the backs of his hands as they lay on his knees in the firelight, and they had seemed rather white and _____; but seeing them now close to me, I could not but notice that they were rather coarse – _____, with squat fingers. Strange to say, there were hairs in the centre of the palm. The nails were _____ and fine, and cut to a sharp point.

Now underline the link verbs in the text.
Can you guess the identity of the character?

15 Choose a famous person, for example a film star, a sports personality, a politician, a TV celebrity.

Write a description of them, including information from these categories:

Physical attributes
hair, eyes, complexion, shape of face, other facial features, build, height, way of walking, gesture, clothes (including size, colour, style and decoration)

Emotional, intellectual and moral attributes
examples: cold, intelligent, dishonest

Habits
behavioural and emotional habits, opinions, gesture and expression

Write your description as if it were from a novel or a screenplay.

Extension and consolidation

Editing

1 An extra word has been added to each line of this extract from *Cider with Rosie* by Laurie Lee. Put a line through the extra word and write it in the space on the right.

When she was about thirteen years old the her mother was taken ill, so the girl had to leave school for the good. She had her five young brothers and her father to look after, and there was but no one else to help it. So she put away her books and her modest ambitions as she was naturally expected to do. The schoolmaster was more furious and called her father as a scoundrel but was helpless to interfere. 'Poor Mr Jolly,' said the Mother, fondly. 'He was never seemed to give up. He used to come round home when I was doing the washing and he lecture me on Oliver Cromwell. He used to sit there so sad, by saying it was a sinful shame, till Father was used to dance and swear ...'

1 _____
2 _____
3 _____
4 _____
5 _____
6 _____
7 _____
8 _____
9 _____
10 _____

Dictation

2 Look at this gapped version of part of the extract from *Mixed Metamessages across Cultures* on page 43 of your Students' Book.

Try to fill in the gaps. Use a pencil.

An American _____ who had _____ for years _____ Japan explained a _____ politeness ethic. _____ lived, as _____ Japanese do, _____ frightfully close _____ – a tiny _____ separated from _____ rooms by _____ walls. In this _____ the walls _____ literally made _____ paper. In _____ to preserve _____ in this _____ unprivate situation, _____ Japanese neighbours _____ acted as _____ no one _____ lived there. _____ never showed _____ of having _____ conversations, and _____, while walking _____ the hall, _____ caught a _____ with the _____ open, they _____ glued their _____ ahead as _____ they were _____ in a _____.

S15 Now listen to a recording of the extract. Complete the extract with the original words.

35

Unit 6

Extensive reading

These extensive reading texts are for your enjoyment rather than for intensive study. Try to avoid using a dictionary while you read. There is an optional exercise at the end.

This is a story from *Dubliners*, a collection of short stories by the Irish writer, James Joyce.

Eveline

She sat at the window watching the evening invade the avenue. Her head was leaned against the window curtains, and in her nostrils was the odour of dusty cretonne. She was tired.

Few people passed. The man out of the last house passed on his way home; she heard his footsteps clacking along the concrete pavement and afterwards crunching on the cinder path before the new red houses. One time there used to be a field there in which they used to play every evening with other people's children. Then a man from Belfast bought the field and built houses in it – not like their little brown houses, but bright brick houses with shining roofs. The children of the avenue used to play together in that field – the Devines, the Waters, the Dunns, little Keogh the cripple, she and her brothers and sisters. Ernest, however, never played: he was too grown up. Her father used often to hunt them in out of the field with his blackthorn stick; but usually little Keogh used to keep *nix* and call out when he saw her father coming. Still they seemed to have been rather happy then. Her father was not so bad then; and besides, her mother was alive. That was a long time ago; she and her brothers and sisters were all grown up; her mother was dead. Lizzie Dunn was dead, too, and the Waters had gone back to England. Everything changes. Now she was going to go away like the others, to leave her home.

Home! She looked round the room, reviewing all its familiar objects which she had dusted once a week for so many years, wondering where on earth all the dust came from. Perhaps she would never see again those familiar objects from which she had never dreamed of being divided. And yet during all those years she had never found out the name of the priest whose yellowing photograph hung on the wall above the broken harmonium beside the coloured print of the promises made to Blessed Margaret Mary Alacoque. He had been a school friend of her father. Whenever he showed the photograph to a visitor her father used to pass it with a casual word:

'He is in Melbourne now.'

She had consented to go away, to leave her home. Was that wise? She tried to weigh each side of the question. In her home anyway she had shelter and food; she had those whom she had known all her life about her. Of course she had to work hard, both in the house and at business. What would they say of her in the Stores when they found out that she had run away with a fellow? Say she was a fool, perhaps; and her place would be filled up by advertisement. Miss Gavan would be glad. She had always had an edge on her, especially whenever there were people listening.

'Miss Hill, don't you see these ladies are waiting?'

'Look lively, Miss Hill, please.'

She would not cry many tears at leaving the Stores.

But in her new home, in a distant unknown country, it would not be like that. Then she would be married – she, Eveline. People would treat her with respect then. She would not be treated as her mother had been. Even now, though she was over nineteen, she sometimes felt herself in danger of her father's violence. She knew it was that that had given her the palpitations. When they were growing up he had never gone for her, like he used to go for Harry and Ernest, because she was a girl; but latterly he had begun to threaten her and say what he would do to her only for her dead mother's sake. And now she had nobody to protect her, Ernest was dead and Harry, who was in the church decorating business, was nearly always down somewhere in the country. Besides, the invariable squabble for money on Saturday nights had begun to weary her unspeakably. She always gave her entire wages – seven shillings – and Harry always sent up what he could, but the trouble was to get any money from her father. He said she used to squander the money, that she had no head, that he wasn't going to give her his hard-earned money to throw about the streets, and much more, for he was usually fairly bad on Saturday night. In the end he would give her the money and ask her had she any intention of buying Sunday's dinner. Then she had to rush out as quickly as she could and do her marketing, holding her black leather purse tightly in her hand as she elbowed her way through the crowds and returning home late under her load of provisions. She had hard work to keep the house together and to see that the two young children who had been left to her charge went to school regularly and got their meals regularly. It was hard work – a hard life – but now that she was about to leave it she did not find it a wholly undesirable life.

She was about to explore another life with Frank. Frank was very kind, manly, open-hearted. She was to go away with him by the night-boat to be his wife and to live with him in Buenos Aires, where he had a home waiting for her. How well she remembered the first time she had seen him; he was lodging in a house on the main road where she used to visit. It seemed a few weeks ago. He was standing at the gate, his peaked cap pushed back on his head and his hair tumbled forward over a face of bronze. Then they had come to know each other. He used to meet her outside the Stores every evening and see her home. He took her to see *The Bohemian Girl* and she felt elated as she sat in an unaccustomed part of the theatre with him. He was awfully fond of music and sang a little. People knew that they were courting, and, when he sang about the lass that loves a sailor, she always felt pleasantly confused. He used to call her Poppens out of fun. First of all it had been an excitement for her to have a fellow and then she had begun to like him. He had tales of distant countries. He had started as a deck boy at a pound a month on a ship of the Allan Line going out to Canada. He told her the names of the ships he had been on and the names of the different services. He had sailed through the Straits of Magellan and he told her stories of the terrible Patagonians. He had fallen on his feet in Buenos Aires, he said, and had come over to the old country just for a holiday. Of course, her father had found out the affair and had forbidden her to have anything to say to him.

'I know these sailor chaps,' he said.

One day he had quarrelled with Frank, and after that she had to meet her lover secretly.

The evening deepened in the avenue. The white of two letters in her lap grew indistinct. One was to Harry; the other was to her father. Ernest had been her favourite, but she liked Harry too. Her father was becoming old lately, she noticed; he would miss her. Sometimes he could be very nice. Not long before, when she had been laid up for a day, he had read her out a ghost story and made toast for her at the fire. Another day, when their mother was alive, they had all gone for a picnic to the Hill of Howth. She remembered her father putting on her mother's bonnet to make the children laugh.

Her time was running out, but she continued to sit by the window, leaning her head against the window curtain, inhaling the odour of dusty cretonne. Down far in the avenue she could hear a street organ playing. She knew the air. Strange that it should come that very night to remind her of the promise to her mother, her promise to keep the home together as long as she could. She remembered the last night of her mother's illness; she was again in the close, dark room at the other side of the hall and outside she heard a melancholy air of Italy. The organ-player had been ordered to go away and given sixpence. She remembered her father coming back into the sick-room saying:

'Damned Italians! coming over here!'

As she mused the pitiful vision of her mother's life laid its spell on the very quick of her being – that life of sacrifices closing in final craziness.

She stood up in a sudden impulse of terror. Escape! She must escape! Frank would save her. He would give her life, perhaps love, too. But she wanted to live. Why should she be unhappy? She had a right to happiness. Frank would take her in his arms, fold her in his arms. He would save her.

*

She stood among the swaying crowd in the station at the North Wall. He held her hand and she knew that he was speaking to her, saying something about the passage over and over again. The station was full of soldiers with brown baggages. Through the wide doors of the sheds she caught a glimpse of the black mass of the boat, lying in beside the quay wall, with illumined portholes. She answered nothing. She felt her cheek pale and cold and, out of a maze of distress, she prayed to God to direct her, to show her what was her duty. The boat blew a long mournful whistle into the mist. If she went, tomorrow she would be on the sea with Frank, steaming towards Bueonos Aires. Their passage had been booked. Could she still draw back after all he had done for her? Her distress awoke a nausea in her body and she kept moving her lips in silent fervent prayer.

A bell clanged upon her heart. She felt him seize her hand:

'Come!'

All the seas of the world tumbled about her heart. He was drawing her into them: he would drown her. She gripped with both hands at the iron railing.

'Come!'

No! No! No! It was impossible. Her hands clutched the iron in frenzy. Amid the seas she sent a cry of anguish.

'Eveline! Evvy!'

He rushed beyond the barrier and called to her to follow. He was shouted at to go on, but he still called to her. She set her white face to him, passive, like a helpless animal. Her eyes gave him no sign of love or farewell or recognition.

7 **Optional exercise.** James Joyce called this story *Eveline*. Can you think of an appropriate alternative title for the story?

Unit 7

Vocabulary development — style

1 Choose the correct alternative to complete these sentences.

1 She has very _____ tastes in clothes and never buys anything from chain stores.
   A ordinary   B sophisticated   C gaudy

2 He's quite an interesting man but his clothes let him down – they're so _____ .
   A scruffy   B frumpy   C unkempt

3 I bought these trousers today – do you think they _____ me?
   A match   B go with   C suit

4 Alice is going to a party tonight. That's why she has _____ .
   A dressed   B undressed   C dressed up

5 Cher is a very stylish woman but occasionally her clothes are a bit _____ – things like see-through black lace blouses and leather dresses, for example.
   A chic   B over the top   C dowdy

6 That's a nice shirt – it _____ the colour of your eyes.
   A matches   B fits   C suits

7 Mountain bikes are very _____ at the moment, but I think it'll pass as they aren't very practical for everyday use.
   A classy   B cosmopolitan   C trendy

8 She's always going through some new _____ ; first it was alternative medicine, then South American dancing, now it's vegetarianism.
   A rage   B craze   C style

Vocabulary building — adjectives ending in -less

On page 54 of your Students' Book you saw the word *tasteless*. The suffix *-less* combines with nouns and verbs to form adjectives in two ways.

A *-less* combines with nouns to form adjectives that describe people or things that do not have or do whatever is referred to.

Note that some adjectives formed in this way are used in a non-literal way. For example, if you describe someone as *brainless*, you mean that they are stupid and silly, not that they have no brain.

B *-less* also combines with nouns or verbs to form adjectives which describe people or things whose qualities cannot be measured in terms of whatever the noun or verb refers to. For example, if a work of art is *priceless*, such as the *Mona Lisa*, it is so valuable that no one can say how much it is worth.

2 Sort the words below into the Categories A and B described above. Use your dictionary.

| characterless   tactless   countless   ageless   timeless |
| hopeless   numberless   powerless   lifeless |

3 Complete these sentences with adjectives from the box above.

1 He really offended his aunt on Sunday by being _____ about her beliefs.

2 Last summer we wanted to have a really exciting holiday, so we went to St Tropez, but there was nothing happening – the place was _____ .

3 When you look around this valley, you can't see a single sign of the twentieth century. You feel that it is _____ .

4 She could be thirteen or thirty years old – she's _____ .

5 Neasden is one of the dullest suburbs of London. Its streets are _____ .

6 When we got to the station the last train had gone, all the hotels were closed, and we had nothing to eat or drink. Our situation seemed _____ .

38

Unit 7

Listening

4 [S16] Listen to Caroline asking Steve about his view of what constitutes style. Which of the four statements below best summarises Steve's philosophy?

A Steve likes fast cars and elegant clothes and sees these as a statement about his own personality.

B Steve likes expensive clothes which help him feel more confident but he doesn't fill his life with electronic gadgets or expensive food.

C Steve thinks that style is about wearing what you want to wear and having a lifestyle not complicated by luxury goods and expensive food and drink.

D Steve says that you should wear anything you want to wear, eat what you want to eat, but pay sufficient attention to other people's opinions.

5 [S16] Read the extracts from the interview below. Some of the words have been wrongly transcribed. Listen again and correct the words that are wrong.

1 ... a lot of people confuse it with money and you know what is fashionable to drive at the moment ...

2 ... I'm really into smart cars and having all mod cons ...

3 ... to have a good lifestyle it's got to be all cars, clothes and food ...

4 ... I don't need to spend twenty pounds on a tin of caviar, that sort of thing ...

5 ... I don't like it when people try and impose their views on me ...

Pronunciation   assimilation (1)

6 [S17] Listen to these sentences. Notice the words with underlining where assimilation takes place.

1 I often find myself in si<u>tu</u>ations where I have to nego<u>ti</u>ate tricky business deals.

2 The museum was full of sen<u>su</u>al sta<u>tu</u>es which Sam appre<u>ci</u>ated enormously.

3 Undergraduates from the School of Educa<u>ti</u>on are often asso<u>ci</u>ated with fa<u>tu</u>ous practical jokes.

4 Eventu<u>a</u>lly there was a return to an appre<u>ci</u>ation of Chris<u>ti</u>an vir<u>tu</u>es.

5 The most important i<u>ss</u>ue in road safety is the use of bi<u>tu</u>men in road repairs.

Now listen and repeat.

Unit 7

Reading

Jackson Browne, the American singer, was once famous for his introspective songs about personal crises, but now things are different …

Read this article from *Q* magazine about how he has changed.

7 In which paragraphs do you find these pieces of information?

A ☐ Evidence that Jackson Browne has become actively involved in protest about political issues.

B ☐ A statement by the singer that he feels he has changed direction over a period of time.

C ☐ An admission that he thinks that his sort of music might not be the best vehicle for protest.

D ☐ A warning that people must become more aware of what they are doing to the planet or risk destroying it.

E ☐ Details of a personal crisis in Jackson Browne's life.

F ☐ A quotation about personal direction from one of his songs.

Phrasal verbs `back`

> In the article about Jackson Browne, the phrasal verb *go back to* is used in the sentence *We can't go back to the land*. The particle *back* is used is many phrasal verbs.

8 Look at the list of meanings below. Which meaning does *back* have in the example sentence above? Write the number of the meaning in the box. ☐

1 returning and movement backwards _____
2 position _____
3 time _____
4 returning or retrieving something _____
5 repeating an action _____
6 control or suppression _____
7 drinking _____

Now match these verbs to the meanings. Use your dictionary if you need help.

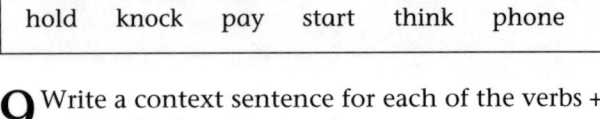

| hold | knock | pay | start | think | phone | drop |

9 Write a context sentence for each of the verbs + particle *back* in Exercise 8.

At a time in his life when he could be taking walk-on parts in *Miami Vice*, Jackson Browne has decided to get dangerous. The one-time chronicler of 'love's illusions', the cute Californian with high-income angst, is using his music to say naughty things about the Presidency, the press and the CIA.

It appears to be a sudden change, but Browne thinks not. He calls it gradual growth. 'I'm ten years older than I was when I recorded *The Pretender* and have less appetite for extreme introspection. At least, I wouldn't want to do a whole album of it.'

The Pretender, produced by Jon Landau, was the consummate statement of his melancholic search for love and meaning. His first wife Phyllis had recently committed suicide and the idealism of the '60s was noticeably giving way to personal concerns of financial security and self-realisation. The title song was a biting epitaph to those who'd waited for a 'great awakening' but who'd eventually surrendered to life as normal.

By the time he toured with it in America during the fall of 1976 he knew he'd mined these themes to exhaustion. More public self-analysis could lead only to self-imitation. Backstage in Washington DC he'd told me, 'I feel I've concluded a certain evaluation, a certain way of looking at things, and I don't care to go back there.'

During the same conversation there were hints of what was to come. He was dismissive about earlier songs in which he'd dreamed about retreating to the desert, avoiding the apocalypse.

But did he still believe in the warnings of songs such as *Before The Deluge* and *The Road And The Sky?* 'The end is nigh? Well, you've got these stockpiles of nuclear waste that have got to sit around for 280,000 years,' he said. 'A dixie cup of it could kill the planet. We can't go back to the land. We've got to grow up. We've got to become a species that cares, or perish. It's as simple as that.'

That Browne has since grown up to become a man who cares, there can be no doubt. He's a passionate critic of North American involvement in Central American politics, has campaigned against nuclear power and nuclear weaponry and has done benefits for various ecological groups. He was part of the *Sun City* record and showed up on the recent Amnesty International tour headlined by Sting and U2.

Those who criticise Browne's new politically conscious material call it 'coffee-table protest'. Is his laid back music the most appropriate vehicle? 'Not really,' he says with an honest laugh. 'But it's the only kind I know how to make.'

For Browne, political campaigning has become a form of salvation. In *The Fuse*, the opening track on *The Pretender*, he'd said that 'the fear of living for nothing strangles the will' and *Running On Empty* was a confession of a man without faith. The search for purpose, disguised in many phrases, has been a persistent Browne theme.

Has his politicisation been more than simply a matter of maturing? Has it fulfilled his quest? 'Ah!', he says, as if found out at last. 'I guess so.' Surely he'd thought about it before? 'Well, I think about it in, er, … yes, I've thought about it a lot. You do want to find the meaning of your life. But in the meantime, life goes on.'

In concert he dedicates one of his songs to a Catholic priest on hunger strike over US involvement in Central America. 'this is for a man who knows what he's doing with his life,' he announced. Is it important to Browne to know what he's doing with his life? 'I'd say it was important to know.' Does he know what he's doing? 'Yeh. And I think it's high time too.'

What is he doing? 'I'm doing what I do best which is to make music. I realise it's all I've ever really known how to do and it's all I want to do but I hope that I'm making music that matters. In other words – and here I'll have to stick my neck out – I want to make a difference.'

Steve Turner

Unit 7

Idioms — words of French origin

The article on page 57 of your Students' Book included some words which are currently used in English but which are of French origin, for example *maître'd* and *de rigueur*.

10 Look at these words of French origin. Match them with their definitions.

1 chic	A	a meeting, often secret, at an agreed place and time
2 de trop	B	a small house or flat for occasional use
3 rendezvous	C	the confidence to do or say the appropriate thing in a social situation
4 laissez-faire	D	fashionable and sophisticated
5 savoir-faire	E	an economic policy based on the idea that governments should not interfere with people's lives
6 pied-à-terre	F	not wanted, because unsuitable or unnecessary in a certain situation

Writing — formal letters – requests

12 Look back at the House of Colour brochure on page 50 of your Students' Book. Imagine that you have decided to improve your image and would like a consultation at the House of Colour.

Write a letter to Alice Prier asking for more information about their work. Observe the conventions for formal letters and use the correct register. You have heard of Alice Prier and House of Colour but you don't know anyone there personally. Include requests for the following information:

- the cost of a consultation
- the length of a consultation
- what a consultation consists of
- opening hours and availability of appointments

Grammar — the article

11 Look at this text from *Punch* magazine. The definite and indefinite articles have been taken out. Replace the articles where necessary.

DESERT WAR

War to stop rapidly spreading desert regions of world is being met head-on by some nations. Israel's systematic pushing back of desert with elaborate irrigation schemes and tree-planting are well-documented. Egypt and such places as Upper Volta are attempting to halt desert expansion by planting 'live fences': hedges of tough desert trees. Oil-rich Libya has come up with bizarre scheme to stop expansion by paving desert. Deep-rooted eucalyptus and acacia trees are planted on dunes. Dunes are sprayed with layer of asphalt in order to stop desert sands from shifting and burying new trees. One of the grandest schemes is current construction of 'Great Green Wall of China': wall of living trees planted roughly parallel to that greatest of planet's man-made structures, ancient stone Great Wall. Green Wall is designed to protect nation from invasion of cold winds and sandstorms that blast out of Siberia and Mongolia which have helped to create vast tracts of desert. Green Wall is part of massive reforestation plan which will result in planting of over quarter-million square miles of trees by year 2000.

Unit 8

Vocabulary development `money`

1 Circle the more appropriate word to complete these sentences.

1 He spends money like **oil/water** – only yesterday he bought ten CDs.
2 Even though I don't earn very much I like to **splash/bash** out once a month and buy some clothes.
3 Look at that car! It's a Chevrolet, isn't it? He must be really **loaded/generous**.
4 When she was a child Annie was very **thrifty/spendthrift** but now she's working, she spends quite a lot.
5 No, I'm sorry, I can't lend you ten pounds – I'm a bit **tight-fisted/hard up** this month.
6 I got a call from my bank telling me that my bank account's in the **red/black** at the moment.
7 Even though it's tempting to use a credit card all the time I find I manage my money better if I pay for everything **by/in** cash.
8 He's a bit **stingy/thrifty** – it's probably because he was very poor as a child.
9 When Mark is feeling a bit low he usually **gives himself/treats himself to** a meal in a good restaurant.
10 In my opinion the other people in my office are rather **tight-fisted/grasping** and spend all their time working out ways of getting more money out of the management.

Vocabulary building `adjectives ending in -able`

> On page 61 of your Students' Book you saw the word *charitable*.
>
> *-able* combines with nouns to form adjectives that describe someone or something as having the qualities or characteristics described by the noun, for example, *fashion – fashionable*.
>
> *-able* also combines with verbs to form adjectives that describe someone or something that is affected by the action or process described by the verb, for example, *read – readable*.
>
> Spelling note: A final *-e* is removed before adding *-able*, except when it comes after a *g* or a *c*. A final *-y* after a consonant is replaced by *i* before adding *-able*. A final *-ate* is replaced by *-able*.

2 Make adjectives ending in *-able* from these nouns and verbs.

enjoy _____   comfort _____
imagine _____ honour _____
identify _____ value _____
vary _____   knowledge _____

3 Use your dictionary to find four other adjectives which end in *-able*. Write a context sentence for each.

Listening `homeless`

4 [S18] Listen to Denis, who used to be one of London's homeless, talk about his early years in the city. Tick the sentences which apply to Denis.

1 ☒ Lived at Centre Point, a hostel.
2 ☒ Couldn't get into hotels because he had no identity papers.
3 ☒ Lived for a year and a half on the streets.
4 ☐ Slept under the bridges over the Thames.
5 ☒ Got money by begging.
6 ☒ Made friends with other people sleeping out.
7 ☒ Worked as a night porter in a hotel.

5 [S18] Listen again and answer these questions.

1 Where does Denis come from originally?
2 Why did he find it difficult to get a job in London?
3 What was Denis's biggest problem sleeping out?
4 Why did he sometimes end up in Dover?
5 What was Denis's attitude to other people on the streets?
6 How did he eventually find work?

Pronunciation `elision`

6 Look at these phrases. Work out whether the letters underlined will be elided or not.

nex<u>t</u> turn	cause<u>d</u> conflict	sof<u>t</u> drink
gues<u>t</u> house	spoil<u>t</u> child	firs<u>t</u> day
las<u>t</u> week	sen<u>d</u> home	Roger <u>h</u>imself
sen<u>d</u> two	serve<u>d</u> tea	nex<u>t</u> day
give <u>h</u>im the book	len<u>t</u> them	I've seen <u>h</u>er twice

Check your answers in the Key.
[S19] Listen and repeat.

Grammar — conditional sentences

7 Incorrect verb tenses are used in some of these sentences. Rewrite the sentences correctly. If there is no mistake, tick the sentence.

1 If you were to go down the High Street today, you didn't recognise it.
2 They would have come to visit you, if they'd known you were at home.
3 If you made a mistake filling in the form, you have to get another one.
4 I wouldn't have invited you if I didn't want to see you.
5 What will you do about unemployment if you were in the government?
6 Whether you would like it or not, Michael Jackson is one of the greatest pop musicians in the world today.
7 Even if there is massive unemployment in the North of England, the South has its problems too.
8 Had they known that Miss Wimblesham was coming, they had sent a car.
9 If you should see Eric later today, tell him to give me a ring.
10 It's a good thing you didn't come to see the play. If you had come, you wouldn't have enjoyed it.

Reading

Look at this article about dogs and a letter written in response to the article.

8 While you read
Think about these questions. What does the writer of the article think of dogs? What sort of person wrote the letter in response to the article?

9 Look at this list of criticisms of dogs. Read the article again and number the ones that the writer mentions in the order that he mentions them.
Dogs …
☐ are often vicious
☐ smell
☐ are not intelligent
☐ are expensive to keep
☐ are ineffective at doing what they are trained to do
☐ make a mess of footpaths and roads
☐ take up a lot of room
☐ are very noisy
☐ are over-affectionate

10 Make a list of the points made to defend dogs in the letter.

SOAPBOX
A curse on meek and mad curs

Graham Noble takes an exceedingly dim view of man's best friend

One of life's enduring mysteries is why so many people like and even dote on dogs. Dogs are dim and smelly and, almost without exception, hopelessly incontinent, rendering paths and parks hazardous to anyone with less than an eagle eye. Many are hyperactive and vicious, barking tirelessly at the least diversion. Those which prefer the peaceful life tend to take up valuable space at the hearth or install themselves in a favoured armchair – casting hairs which cling to clothes with great tenacity – and fawn embarrassingly on anyone who will pat them. All of them, meek or mad, cost the earth in food and vets' bills. So-called working dogs are little better. Sheepdogs are notoriously incompetent, requiring the shepherd to whistle and shout commands until he is blue in the face. Then there are police sniffer dogs, charged with seeking out drugs and explosives. Are they so different from pet dogs in that they sniff more than each others' behinds with any enthusiasm? As for guard dogs, surely a gaggle of handsome geese does the job more effectively and with less fuss? Dogs have had their day.

Hound bites back over canine slur

GRRR! I take strong exception, as I'm sure most of my canine friends do, to Graham Noble's Soapbox ("A curse on meek and mad curs", Sept. 20). I am neither vicious nor incontinent but if I ever meet your resident dog-hater, nothing would give me greater pleasure than sinking my teeth into Mr Nobel. Before this bigot vents his fury any further, perhaps he should compare our faults with those of his own species. Do we massacre the environment? Do we rob, steal and rape? I agree with Mr Noble on one score. I would hate to be locked all day in some dilapidated inner-city flat with no nice smells and nowhere to roam.

Humans don't have a right to treat us like that. We give pleasure to millions; we make life bearable for humans who cannot see. As our sense of smell is a million times stronger than Mr Noble's, think how badly he must smell to us. This gift does, of course, enable us to help mankind by locating dangerous drugs. Dogs have been on this Earth as long as Mr Noble's ancestors; we have every intention of staying.
Finlay
(bearded collie)
Hertfordshire, England

There're only two Ns in canine

Unit 8

Idioms `cost`

> In the article about dogs, the writer used the expression *cost the earth*, which means 'cost a lot of money'.

11 Four of these expressions are genuine and three are not. Which ones?
Two of the genuine expressions are slang. Which ones?
Use your dictionary to help you.

cost a belt of money
cost a small fortune
cost a truckload
cost a mint
cost a packet
cost a bomb
cost a politician's wages

Phrasal verbs `on`

> In the article about dogs, the phrasal verb *dote on* is used, meaning 'show a great deal of love and care towards someone to an extent which other people consider excessive.' The particle *on* is used in many other phrasal verbs.

12 Match the meanings to the verbs. Use your dictionary to help you.

1 continuation	A expand on
2 depending and expecting	B chance on
3 focusing, effects, actions and feelings	C cheer on
4 attacking	D hold on
5 progress and encouragement	E count on
6 discovery	F dote on
7 subjects and topics	G turn on

13 Use the verbs in Exercise 12 to complete these sentences.
1 Do you mind _____ on while I go and turn off the oven?
2 I _____ on a beautiful old vase when I was at the market last week.
3 She really _____ on this man that she met a couple of weeks ago.
4 I thought the dog looked quite docile but when I approached him he _____ on me and bit my hand.
5 We're really _____ on your support at the next election, you know.
6 The crowd _____ on England but Wales scored two tries in the last five minutes.
7 Dr Morris _____ on the subject of AIDS in response to a question from the audience.

Grammar `inversion`

14 Look back at the expressions in Exercise 1 on page 66 of your Students' Book. Make these sentences more emphatic in the same way.
1 The painting was beautiful. I wanted to buy it.
2 I left the building. It started to rain.
3 I stepped into the bath. The doorbell rang.
4 Kathy works as a teacher. She also writes children's fiction.
5 My cat, Elvis, is very fat. He can no longer get in through the cat flap.
6 It was the most interesting journey I've ever made.
7 I didn't notice the flat tyre until I tried to drive off.
8 I refuse to do overtime unless you pay me double the hourly rate.

Writing `story writing`

15 Think of a traditional story or fable from your culture that everyone knows.

Write an up-dated version of the story, setting it in modern times, giving the characters appropriate names, jobs, social backgrounds, and so on. Observe the conventions of story-telling.

Extension and consolidation

Editing

1 There are deliberate errors of layout, punctuation, paragraphing and spelling in this letter to *The Big Issue*. Rewrite it correcting the errors.

A friend in need

> Dear John.
>
> Yesterday I went to a job inteview in South Kensington, when I left the wether was awful, it was pouring with rain, and the wind was blowing cold and hard.
>
>   I walked to the tube but when I cam to buy my ticket I had no money, I had lost it.
>
>   The only way home was to walk. I came out of the tube, about to start wolking in the rain, and asked the guy who sells The Big Issue outside the station which way it was to Oxford Street. He reelised my misfortune and dug in his pocket and gave me a pound, enouff to get me home.
>
>   I'd just like to say that I do buy The Big Issue in aid of helping the homeles and I am stunned that; when the tables were turned, someone less fortunate than myself was eager to help,
>
>   Thanks to the guy from South Kensington.
>
>   Yours faithfully
>
>   Soraya

Dictation

2 [S20] Look at these unfinished sentences from the article on page 65 of your Students' Book. Listen and complete the sentences.

1 More fortunate than Ruffian is Rosemary, an angora rabbit _____
_____

2 To call Rosemary's garden dwelling a 'hutch' would _____
_____

3 Its complex construction _____
_____

4 Built from timber, it is over eight feet in length, _____
_____

5 The front door is decorated with an eye, a heart and a rabbit to signify _____
_____

6 The interior boasts walls decorated with _____
_____

7 If the temperature falls too low in winter, _____
_____

Unit 8

Extensive reading

These extensive reading texts are for your enjoyment rather than for intensive study. Try to avoid using a dictionary while you read. There is an optional exercise at the end.

This is a short story called *The Small Horse* by a British writer, Steve Walker.

I thought it was a mouse at first, and wasn't bothered. Living in a place like this, one must expect the odd mouse. True: it whinnied in the night and woke me up more than once. I climbed out of bed, pulled back the curtains and looked through sleepy eyes at the closed warehouse over the road. I thought the whinnies came from there. True, also: it clip-clopped behind the skirting-board, just like a horse would if horses were small. But I didn't think of that. I took it to be a heavy-footed rodent.

I first saw it one Sunday tea-time – the most miserable time of the week for me; I turn off the TV to avoid the religious programmes and, left with nothing to do, I become miserable: always do. I was buttering some bread when I head horses' noises. I glanced. Wow! There it was, hoofing the lino by the larder door. A small horse! No larger, indeed, than an underfed mouse – ribs showing, eyes popping. I watched it carefully, stood still with bread in one hand and knife with a scoop of butter on it in the other. Yes, it was certainly, most definitely, a horse, a small horse.

I must say, I've always been the same, ever since I passed twenty. I used to be a songwriter then, or thought I was, but all my songs had been turned down and I was at breaking point. Nothing whatsoever had gone right for me. I'd recently started my present job, and told a salesman I worked with about my problem.

'Give it up,' he jeered at me. 'You've got a good job here. Give it up. You'll never make it.'

What he really meant was: You're an ordinary bloke, like me. You've no business thinking you're a songwriter. People like us aren't songwriters.

He was correct, of course. I followed his advice, but note now that ever since, it seems to me, I've avoided people and things that could be judged as being out of the ordinary. So what was I to do when confronted with the crisis of having a small horse infesting my flat? I needed advice, but only knew ordinary people. I told one or two and they said: 'Come on, man – stop pulling our leg.' And they proceeded to avoid me for the next few days.

I told Mr Ducksbury, my sales-manager. He reacted the same, then started showing me new photos of his grandchildren.

'No. No. Really. I'm serious,' I said.

'Oh, yeah. A small horse? There's no such thing.'

'But there is – I've seen one.'

'Then why's no one else ever seen one? What makes you so special?'

There was a young man who'd worked part-time in the packing department for a bit. I'd avoided talking to him at the time, even when I needed to check on a stock-level, because someone had said he was a painter – oils and all that. I looked up his address in the files. It was near one of my calls – I went there that very day.

'Excuse me.'

'Yes.'

'You may remember me from Hollis's. Can I come in for a moment?'

He let me in.

There were two naked girls seated back to back on a dais thing. He was painting them, all in orange. I was highly embarrassed. One put on a dressing-gown and went to make a pot of tea, but the other just sat there scratching herself. I never got the tea, and didn't gabble through much of my story to the young man, either. He grew sarcastic very quickly and asked me to leave. The girls started laughing as he prodded me out.

When I got back home the horse was drinking from a saucer of milk I'd left out for it. I poured some breakfast cereal into my hand and offered it for the thing to eat. It stood thinking, but wouldn't dare come. I got bored of crouching there, so went off to watch TV.

But I tried to get it to eat from my hand every time I saw it and, at last, a fortnight later, mid-morning – I hadn't bothered to go to work – it trotted up and ate contentedly from my hand. I was thrilled to see it close up. With my feeding, it had put on some weight. What a perfect little thing it was! But, being the way I am, I couldn't tolerate its mystery, its extraordinariness. I decided to kill it, to put poison down and be rid of it.

As soon as this thought entered my mind, the horse gave me a quick look, reared, and galloped away. I pulled off my shoe and threw it after. But my aim was bad; the horse disappeared unharmed through the hole where the plug used to be when I had the old fridge.

A few nights later, I woke up scared. A dream, I thought, already forgotten – or was the horse in my bedroom? I was suddenly petrified of it, as if it were a spider. I searched the bedsheets, looked under the furniture, checked the skirting-board for cracks, new or old. Nothing. Once again I pulled back the curtains to look at that closed warehouse over the road. I'd always

 had my suspicions about it, and this time it could be tiny lights shining behind the filthy grilled windows at pavement level.

I got dressed at once, put a torch in my pocket and hurried over. I stood right in front of the grilled windows – but they were too filthy; I couldn't see anything through them.

There was an old door there, on crusty hinges. I kicked it open, two kicks. I switched on my torch and went inside. I was in a foreman's office: cabinets, desk and such still there. A twelve-year-old calendar was on the wall.

I listened. Yes – a mouse-like scratching. This was surely where my small horse had come from, and maybe, I figured, there'd be a whole herd in the warehouse somewhere.

In the light from my torch nothing had any colour. I walked on battered floorboards towards the main storeroom. A tall, wooden sliding door barred my way. I could find no handle and my pushing and coaxing wouldn't budge the thing. I gave it a kick but it was thick and solid and didn't feel it.

What else could I do? I gave up and turned to go. But after only a few steps, I heard the sliding door open behind me. I jumped in fright. Had I pressed a button without realizing it? Was there someone there?

I shone my torch. It flitted across a huge ceiling, showing smashed skylights with the night above. Then I waved it around the warehouse floor.

There were horses, yes, quite a few, just like the one in my flat. But also, everywhere, as if assembled to witness some spectacular event, were people, tiny people. Thousands and thousands of them – all just as tall as a little finger. Most were naked, some wore paper hats and carried spears of broken glass. Lots of them were huddled around little fires they'd made. They stood still in my torchlight, but where my torch couldn't catch, some were running.

I'm home now, in bed with the light on. I'm going to sit up all night reading the Bible out loud.

3 Optional exercise. What do you think of the events described in the story?

Do you think the protagonist is mad?
Write a sixteen-word summary of the story.

Unit 9

Vocabulary development — the home

1 Look at these pairs of words. Which type of accommodation would you prefer in each case and why?

Example: caravan/tent
I would prefer to spend my holidays in a caravan rather than in a tent. Caravans are more convenient. Caravans are better if the weather is bad. And I find it difficult to sleep in a sleeping bag.

1 caravan/tent
2 house/bungalow
3 hotel/motel
4 bedsit/flat
5 detached house/semi-detached house
6 flat/maisonette

Vocabulary building — nouns ending in -er

On page 70 of your Students' Book you saw the words *cabin cruiser*, *camper* and *trailer*. *-er* combines with verbs to form nouns that refer to things rather than people. For example, a *computer* is an electronic machine that can perform computations and that stores and retrieves information.

-er also combines with verbs to form nouns that refer to people who do the action described by the original verb, usually because it is their job. For example, a *lecturer* is someone who *lectures*; a *teacher* is someone who *teaches*.

2 Look at these verbs. Convert them into nouns ending in *-er* and put them under the appropriate heading below.

| paint | cook | record | dust | farm | wait | mix |
| photograph | | blend | | manage | | |

people	objects

Now write a definition for each noun.

Phrasal verbs — away

In the conversation about living on a boat on page 71, you heard Helen say *you have to pack it all away and put it away again* ... The particle *away* here corresponds to the meaning 'storing, hiding and isolating' listed below. As well as its literal use to indicate movement, *away* has six other meanings in phrasal verbs.

3 Match the verbs to the meanings below. There are two verbs for each meaning. Use your dictionary if you need help.

1 withdrawal and non-involvement
2 removal, transfer and separation
3 storing, hiding and isolating
4 getting rid of and destroying things
5 disappearance
6 continuous activity

slog away
explain away
clear away
run away
take away
work away
melt away
wash away
call away
tuck away
keep away
wear away

4 Choose one of the verbs for each meaning and write a context sentence.

Listening

5 [S21] Listen to Tony talking about an unpleasant experience he had when he was sharing a flat. Make notes about Tony's flatmate's room.

Write a description of Tony's flatmate's room based on your notes.

Pronunciation `phrasal verbs`

6 Underline the phrasal verb particles in these sentences which you think will be accented.

1 I woke my sister up, then went and had breakfast.
2 They always got up late on Sundays, never before midday.
3 Turn off the TV, will you? It's getting on my nerves.
4 You can come in now, Henry.
5 Come in. I'm sorry to have kept you waiting.
6 He switched on the engines and the plane took off.

[S22] Now listen and check your answers. Then listen and repeat.

Reading

This article from the *Independent* describes the life of Tricia Parrott, a signwriter who lives on a houseboat in London.

7 Before you read

Below are the opening sentences from seven of the paragraphs in the text. They are wrongly ordered. Can you predict the correct order? Number the left-hand column of boxes.

☐☐ Ms Parrott says she cannot afford to be materialistic.

☐☐ So they sold everything and bought a narrowboat.

☐☐ 'I don't mind if people glance through the window,' says Tricia Parrott, looking out at the path alongside her home.

☐☐ 'It's like living in a linear village,' she says.

☐☐ What most people might mind about Ms Parrott's way of life is the inconvenience.

☐☐ What she and her husband gave up 20 years ago was a two-bedroom flat in Holland Park, west London.

☐☐ Ms Parrott, 57, has lived on the barge for eight years (alone, for the past two, since the death of her husband, Eric, a schoolteacher) and for 12 years before that on a narrowboat on the same mooring.

8 While you read

Read the article and find the actual location of the sentences above. Number the right-hand column of boxes. Was your ordering correct?

9 Read the text again and find five reasons why Tricia Parrott has chosen to live on a houseboat.

Unit 9

Casting off from the easy life

'I DON'T mind if people glance through the window,' says Tricia Parrott, looking out at the path alongside her home. 'But I get annoyed when they stick their faces up against the glass.'

You can sympathise with the nosey. Ms Parrott's home does attract more attention than most. The names of her neighbours' homes, 'Foxy Lady', 'Insayn Jayne' and 'The Scarlet Pimpernel', might give you a clue to her mode of residence. These are the brightly coloured narrowboats moored on the stretch of water between Little Venice and Regent's Park known as Broadwater. And nestling in among them is Ms Parrott's large Dutch barge, *Ons Verlangen* (Our Dream).

Ms Parrott, 57, has lived on the barge for eight years (alone, for the past two, since the death of her husband, Eric, a schoolteacher) and for 12 years before that on a narrowboat at the same mooring. She likes people to know it is her only home, and that she works – as a sign painter and teacher of signwriting – to maintain it. She is also keen that life on the water is properly represented.

'Some people pay a lot of money for their moorings because they think living on the canals will be romantic,' she says as she sits stroking her large black cat, Tiger, in her sitting-cum-breakfast-cum-classroom. 'Which it is. And it is mentally relaxing. But what they don't realise is that there is a lot of muck. Physically, it is a very hard life. We made a definite choice. We knew what we were giving up and what we were gaining.'

What she and her husband gave up 20 years ago was a two-bedroom flat in Holland Park, west London. Although they had spent their honeymoon on the Norfolk Broads ('I'd always liked boating but never fancied the Cowes lot'), it was only when their seven-year-old son, Toby, needed building up after an illness that they decided to buy themselves a 24ft cruiser.

They spent the six weeks of Eric's school holiday that summer on the canals. 'For the next three years we spent every moment we could on the water and we fell in love with the painted boats. We were hooked by the magic of it all, the light shining off the water and reflected in the roof, the freedom, the camaraderie. It fitted our lifestyle very well. I learnt to paint the roses and castles you associate with narrowboats, and my husband took his typewriter and wrote.

'Weatherwise, those summers were awful, but it didn't matter. We thought if we can spend six weeks in the rain and not be at each other's throats, we can live that way all the time. It seemed logical we should move permanently on to the water.'

So they sold everything and bought a narrowboat. It was not cheap; her barge cost £60,000 to buy and convert, and she pays £2,000 a year for her licence and rent, not to mention the poll tax.

'The only things we took with us were some oak unit bookcases which we used to make walls. And, of course, we used them to store books. Everything has to have a dual purpose. Your sofa has to be comfortable and have storage space underneath. You use your airing cupboard for raising bread. Normal furniture doesn't fit in to a narrowboat. There is not enough space.'

But that does not worry Ms Parrott. 'I like things to be busy and happening,' she says. It was particularly busy and happening when they were bringing up Toby on board. She has no qualms about small children living so close to water. 'Once they learn to swim it's no problem,' she says. 'And when they are tiny you just chain the carrycot to the roof when you are cruising. They get plenty of fresh air.' So enamoured with the waterway lifestyle was Toby that he now earns his living building boats.

Although Ms Parrott is now alone, the clutter has not subsided. 'It gets chaotic, but I love it. I like corners where I can

49

Unit 9

tuck myself away. If I want space, I simply go outside. Living on a boat, you have the prospect of moving, and that gives you all the mental space in the world.'

What most people might mind about Ms Parrott's way of life is the inconvenience. Now she is linked to the mains, so she has telephone, television and electric lighting when moored. But in the past she had to run the engine to charge the batteries; once when the pipes froze she washed with melted snow that she scraped off the boat's roof. She still has to have a postbox at the local post office, as the security door that leads from the bridge to the canal towpath is locked at night, preventing early morning deliveries.

But the major inconvenience is the convenience. Going to the lavatory involves pumping, priming and pumping again. The water tank has to be filled by hose at least once a week, and emptying the sewage tank means a trip to Little Venice, where there are special sanitary points where the stuff can be pumped into the main sewage system (an exercise US water-dwellers refer to as 'emptying the honey-pot'). 'You can just catch a whiff of methane now,' she laughs. 'That means the tank is full.'

Ms Parrott says she cannot afford to be materialistic. 'Your priority is to be able to get out to the country, to the magic of the waterways. So getting your engine mended is always more important than a washing machine. It's not a luxurious life. One of the first things you learn is the water you wash with is also used to clean the floor. When you've only got a 10-gallon water tank you have to be economical. It's like camping – larking about and having fun. I have always felt that as long as you can keep clean, eat good food and have comfortable beds, the rest you can cope with.'

And the rest does go on. The break-ins, the theft and the occasional dead bodies – a grim side of life about which Ms Parrott is matter-of-fact. 'It's what you pay for your freedom. For being able just to cast off and go and see a play at Stratford or friends in Worcester.'

Her conversation is peppered with references of admiration to her late husband. But since his death she claims her life has not been empty, precisely because of where she lives.

'It's like living in a linear village,' she says. 'I've got a network of friends and as boats go up and down they carry news from one to the other. There's always lots to do, so there's no time to mope. And if you feel depressed, the water is very soothing.'

Idioms   birds

In the article about Tricia Parrott, the expression *larking about* is used. To *lark about* means to enjoy yourself by doing silly or naughty things. Bird names are often used in idiomatic expressions in English.

10 Use these names of birds to complete the sentences below (each one is used twice).

| lark | chicken | duck | crow |

1 The other boy was bigger than me and I was too _____ to fight him.

2 She reminded Matthew that he had to be in the office by nine every day, but it was like water off a _____ 's back and he just carried on as before.

3 Anna took to skiing like a _____ to water.

4 I think he's a real bore. OK, he's successful but he needn't go round _____ about it.

5 We were up with the _____ this morning and were on the road by eight o'clock.

6 The management promised us a pay rise in the near future but we're not counting our _____ before they're hatched as they've promised one before.

7 It's about 50 miles from London to Brighton as the _____ flies.

8 We went to Alton Towers fairground for a _____ and it was great fun!

Unit 9

Grammar — question tags

11 Some of these questions have the wrong tag. Correct the tags if necessary and make up possible answers to each question.

1. I'm going the right way, aren't I?
2. You will remember to write, will you?
3. Michael Jackson has gone completely white, didn't he?
4. You are enjoying your English course, don't you?
5. I really like house music, don't you?
6. I'll tell you what I'm going to do, will I?
7. Shut the door, will you?
8. You won't tell anyone else about this, will you?
9. You went to that restaurant last week, didn't you?
10. Let's stop here, shall we?

12 Make up a main clause about the topic in brackets to fit these question tags.

1. (politics) …, isn't he?
2. (pets) …, aren't they?
3. (personality) …, aren't I?
4. (food) …, don't you?
5. (city life) …, aren't there?
6. (sport) …, don't they?
7. (education) …, did you?
8. (travel experience) …, have you?
9. (studying a foreign language) …, doesn't it?
10. (environmental problems) …, isn't it?

non-defining relative clauses

13 Join these pairs of sentences to make one sentence, using a relative pronoun.

Example: I met William's brother. He's an airline pilot.
    I met William's brother who's an airline pilot.

1. Bristol is in the west of England. It is a busy university city.
2. This is Alison. I lived on her boat this summer.
3. I spent all my money. This annoyed my wife enormously.
4. There was a group of football supporters on our train. One of them jumped out while the train was still moving.
5. We are going to Galicia for our holidays. Galicia is in the north-west of Spain.
6. They gave me three cassettes for Christmas. I already had two of them.
7. Chet Baker died in 1992. He was a famous jazz trumpet player.

defining relative clauses

14 Complete these sentences with a relative clause.

Example: The plane leaves at 10.50./She's too late to catch the plane *that leaves at 10.50.*

1. Her car was stolen./Have the police found the car _____?
2. I heard a new record last week./I didn't really enjoy the new record _____.
3. We bought an interesting painting when we were on holiday./Have you seen the interesting painting _____?
4. A bicycle was vandalised outside the school./The bicycle _____ belongs to the new French teacher.
5. Robert Capa took this photograph in 1942./This is one of the photographs _____.
6. The doctor's secretary came to the door./The doctor's secretary _____ told me the doctor was out.
7. You hear a lot of gossip in the canteen./You shouldn't believe all the gossip _____.

Writing — composition

15 Choose a topic. Write a composition about it. Look at the composition features revised on page 77 of your Students' Book. Make a plan before you write. Hand it in with your finished composition.

- Animals are for the service of humanity.
- Nobody should have to take an HIV test.
- The United Nations peacekeeping force is a complete waste of time.
- Shakespeare was the greatest playwright of his time.
- Property is theft.
- The quality of pop music has got gradually worse over the last ten years.
- TV advertising interferes with enjoyment of programmes.
- I'm the most intelligent student in this class.
- Animals exist for the service of humanity.
- There will be a major war in Europe in the next twenty years.
- We'd all be happier if we had more money.

Unit 10

Vocabulary development — moods

1 Without looking at page 78 of your Students' Book, write:

1 five expressions which mean 'to be depressed'.
2 three expressions which mean 'to feel happy'.
3 three expressions which describe a person's character.
4 three ways of dealing with someone who is depressed.

Now use one expression from each category to write sentences about people you know and their moods.

2 Complete these sentences explaining how you cope with moods.

1 When I'm feeling down in the dumps ...
2 When a friend of mine is in a foul mood ...
3 When a colleague is very irritable ...
4 When I want to snap out of a bad mood ...
5 When I'm feeling on top of the world ...
6 When a member of my family is in a bad temper ...
7 When I want to cheer a friend up ...

Vocabulary building — degrees of colour

As you saw on page 79 of your Students' Book, there are not many words to describe colour in English. *-ish* and *-y* are added to some adjectives when we are not sure of a colour or when the colour is not very strong or definite. When an adjective formed in this way is followed by another colour, for example *pinky red*, the first adjective, *pinky*, indicates the particular shade of the second colour, *red*.

Spelling note: A final *-e* is replaced by *-ish* or *-y*. If a word of one syllable ends in a *-b, -d, -g, -t* or *-n* preceded by a single vowel, the *b, d, g, t* or *n* is doubled before adding *-ish* or *-y*.

3 Make likely combinations of adjectives from these pairs of colours.

1 white/blue _____
2 blue/black _____
3 green/yellow _____
4 red/purple _____
5 brown/red _____
6 purple/maroon _____

Now add a suitable noun to each adjective combination.

Example: *a brownish red house*

Listening

4 [S23] Read the statements below carefully. Listen to the conversation between Joanne and Johnathan. Decide which statements are true and which are false.

1 ☐ Johnathan says he sometimes gets very depressed for long periods.
2 ☐ Johnathan says his girlfriend sometimes gets depressed.
3 ☐ He says that you have to give depressed people time to get over their depression.
4 ☐ He has no experience of dealing with clinically depressed people.
5 ☐ He thinks that two weeks would be a reasonable time to put up with another person's depression.
6 ☐ He mentions a very depressed person he knew at school.
7 ☐ He can't remember ever seeing this person happy.

5 [S23] Listen again and complete these sentences from the conversation.

1 I don't think I tend to ...
2 I mean, like my girlfriend ...
3 I wouldn't know how to deal with it if ...
4 I remember living with ...
5 Yeah, I don't think...

Idioms `ear`

> In the conversation between Joanne and Johnathan you heard Johnathan say that he *played it by ear*. This means that he decided what to do by responding to events as they happened rather than by following a plan.

6 Look at the word *ear* used in these sentences. Work out a definition for each expression.

1 Tell me all about what happened at the meeting – I'm **all ears**.

2 Look at that man at the next table! His **ears are flapping**! I wish he'd mind his own business – this doesn't concern him.

3 Don't you ever listen? Whatever I say, it goes **in one ear and out the other**.

4 I like to **keep my ear to the ground** at this time of year when the management are discussing the annual pay deal.

5 If you cause any trouble here, you'll be **out on your ear**.

6 I'll give him **a thick ear** if he ever says anything as rude as that again.

7 Motorists have **turned a deaf ear** to the police campaign to leave their cars at home on foggy days.

Pronunciation `linking r`

7 Look at the letter *r* where it comes at the end of a word in these sentences. Decide whether it is pronounced or not. Underline the *r*s that are pronounced.

1 I don't think I tend to get depressed for very long.

2 I mean, what do you do to help her?

3 ... you just play it by ear and could be a week, could be two weeks you just have to realise that you know they're going to be negative for a couple of days about or however long and then you know sort of gradually they'll get over it.

S24 Now listen and check your answers.

Reading

8 Read this text about the Lüscher colour test very quickly and answer these questions.

1 What is the purpose of the test?

2 What does the test consist of?

3 Who is the test particularly useful for?

The Lüscher Test

In stating preferences for this colour or for that, choice is often dictated by circumstances. If the circumstances are the choice of a dress to wear, a wallpaper for the living-room, a paint for the kitchen cupboards, then the resultant choice is determined not only by psychological preference or physiological need (though these will inevitably play a part), but by aesthetic considerations: will the dress go with general colouring or figure? what does the wallpaper do to the curtains and furniture? and so forth.

When, as in the Lüscher Test, colours are presented for choice without involvement of one with the other, then aesthetic judgement becomes subordinate to personal preference, with no need to try to harmonize them with one another, nor to refer the colours to some other frame of reference. It is desirable, just the same, when the test is being given to someone else to suggest that the colours should be selected just as colours, without mental value-judgements as to their suitability for dress materials, furnishings or the upholstery of a new automobile.

In the 'Full' Lüscher Test there are seven different panels of colours, containing in all seventy-three colour-patches, consisting of twenty-five different hues and shades, and requiring forty-three different selections to be made. The resulting test-protocol affords a wealth of information concerning the conscious and unconscious psychological structure of the individual, areas of psychic stress, the state of glandular balance or imbalance, and much physiological information of great value either to the physician or to the psychotherapist. The complete test takes only five to eight minutes, which makes it probably the speediest test on record, while its administration is so simple that it can be taught to almost anyone in half an hour. However, the interpretation of the Full Test requires training and considerable psychological insight. For this reason, this 'Introduction' includes only one of the seven panels – the so-called 'Eight-colour Panel'.

This shortened version of the test is known as the 'Quick Test' or the 'Short Lüscher Test' and though not nearly so comprehensive nor so revelatory as the Full Test, it is still of considerable value in highlighting significant aspects of the personality, and in drawing attention to areas of psychological and physiological stress where they exist. Physicians in Europe use this short version of the test as a useful aid to diagnosis, since it has been found that such stresses show up in the Lüscher Test often long before their physiological results make themselves evident; in this, the test provides them with an incomparable 'early warning system' of stress ailments in their early stages – ailments such as cardiac malfunction, cerebral attack or disorders of the gastro-intestinal tract.

The physician is a busy man who has little time to spare for diagnostic media additional to those which are his normal complement, nor for the learning of complicated methods of test interpretation. With the Short Lüscher Test he can with little trouble assign the actual administration of the test to his nurse-receptionist, and with a little practice on his own part tell at a glance whether his patient has a normal test or whether there are signs of stress in areas which should be further investigated.

Unit 10

9
Read the text about the Lüscher Test again and write a sentence about each of these topics.

1. How we choose colours in everyday life.
2. How people should select the colours in the test.
3. The Full Lüscher colour test.
4. The Short Lüscher Test.
5. The use of the test as an 'early warning system'.
6. Doctors, nurses and the test.

Phrasal verbs show

In the text about the Lüscher Test, the phrasal verb *show up* is used, meaning 'to be made noticeable as part of the result of an experiment'.

10
The verb *show* is used with other particles in phrasal verbs. Circle the correct particle in these sentences.

1. A woman came to the door and showed me **out/in**.
2. Orange is a good colour for life-jackets because it shows **up/down** against the green of the sea.
3. Bill is a good diver and he likes showing **off/out** when people are watching.
4. We were shown **around/through** the new flat by a very pleasant woman from the estate agent's.
5. His anger about the proposed new road showed **through/off** right from the beginning of the meeting.
6. I was outside the Town Hall at six o'clock as agreed but none of the others showed **down/up**.
7. Our children really showed us **round/up** last weekend by eating more than anyone else at the party.
8. Jill showed samples of the new curtain material **through/around** the office and most people liked it.

Now check your answers in your dictionary.

Grammar modal verbs

11
The wrong modal verbs have been used in some of these sentences. Identify the ones which are wrong and rewrite them using the correct verbs.

1. He didn't have a car so he shan't have driven home.
2. This isn't Conkreton, we can't have taken the wrong road.
3. She had to catch the seven o'clock plane.
4. A week after he had the operation he may return to work.
5. She must stop working so hard or she'll make herself ill.
6. Shall you give me an envelope, please?
7. They needn't plan their holiday last year because their parents booked everything for them.
8. If we hurry, we should be there by lunchtime.
9. They must be coming to the party, but I'm not sure.
10. You might go home early today, if you want to.

12
For a number of years these so-called 'crop circles' have appeared in fields around Britain. Many hypotheses have been put forward to explain their presence. Use these verbs to make hypotheses of your own about them.

could (have)	might (have)	must (have)
may (have)	can't (have)	

Now use these verbs to make suggestions about what the investigators should do to find out what they really are.

could	should	can	ought to

54

Unit 10

Writing

Look at this extract from a guide to restaurants at Euro Disney featured in a London listings magazine:

> Alternatively, try breakfast at the Chuckwagon Café (Hotel Cheyenne) – the best place we found for a reasonably priced slap-up Disney hotel breakfast. Self-service counters and dishes include steaming porridge for 25F which will certainly set you up for the day.

Notice that the style of the review is informal and that the writer uses words and expressions which would normally be found in spoken English. This is characteristic of magazine journalism.

13 Write a guide to the restaurants, cafés, bars and so on in your area. Include descriptions of about four or five places. Copy the style of the extract above.

Extension and consolidation

Editing

1 This text is about the use of the colour white in interior decorating. There is a word missing from each line. Put an asterisk (*) in the text to show where the word is missing and write the word in the space on the right.

I used think white is white is white. But as with every other colour, there are dozens of different shades. And I've come realise that the warmer tones my favourites.
  In saying this, I'm influenced by latest trends. The creamy white of unbleached cotton and the powdery bloom of stone big news in decorating, thanks to our growing preference for simplicity natural materials. But it also feels right. Just as there are days only a snowy white shirt will do, so are times when it's the only colour I'm prepared to consider when I look towels or china.
  However, there nothing faddy about decorating with warm whites. On the contrary, I can't think of more timeless approach. Freeing yourself from anxieties surround colour (What if I hate it? How will it look on a dreary winter's day?) gives you a chance escape the tyranny of decorating trends. You longer have to worry about splashy wallpapers looking dated two years' time, or whether you'll be able to live with lime green upholstery for the rest your days.

1 _____
2 _____
3 _____
4 _____
5 _____
6 _____
7 _____
8 _____
9 _____
10 _____
11 _____
12 _____
13 _____
14 _____
15 _____
16 _____

Dictation

2 Below are parts of sentences taken from the text you read on page 75 of your Students' Book. You are given the first and last words and a word from the middle.

S25 Listen to the whole text. Reconstruct the sentences. Play the tape again. You are allowed to play the tape as many times as you like but you are not allowed to stop it after each sentence.

1 It's ... way ... away.

2 Don't ... stuff ... more.

3 Go ... radio ... contemplate.

4 Some ... come ... reflex.

5 You ... and you ... pain.

Unit 10

Improve your language learning

appropriacy (2) writing

3 Look at this list of different types of text. Find an example of each type of text below. Write the letters in the boxes. (One of the texts does not belong to any any of the categories.)

1. ☐ instructions for use of medicine
2. ☐ film review
3. ☐ postcard
4. ☐ novel
5. ☐ guarantee
6. ☐ advertisement
7. ☐ service manual
8. ☐ tourist guide
9. ☐ formal letter

D ABROAD / SEND FOR OUR NEW 1993 BROCHURE / HIGH PLACES / ICELAND FOR REAL ADVENTURERS! / Trek, hike, backpack, ski in fjord mountains, volcanoes, glaciers, canyons & snow! / High Places Ltd, Globe Works Penistone Rd., Sheffield S6 3AE / Telephone 0742 757500 24hrs / ATOL 2836 Fully Bonded

E Dear Reader,
Thank you for your annual subscription to BBC ... the enclosed issue. We will be sending you a ... our next subscription is due.
ase make a note of your reference ... to be found above your name ...

F ...arbour & Sons Ltd, undertake that, for a period ... months after the purchase of one of their products, should any fault arise due to faulty materials or workmanship, they will, at their discretion, repair or replace the defective part.
This guarantee does not apply to faults caused by misuse, excessive wear and tear, accidents or alterations to the product carried out by persons other than the manufacturer. It is also invalid if the product has not been worn and looked after in accordance with the ... instructions supplied.
This guarantee applies to the original purchase ... and is given in addition to your statutory rights.
In the unlikely event of any complaint, please retu... to your dealer; or in the case of difficulty, to us, ... date and place of purchase and nature ...
J. Barbour & Sons Ltd, Customer ... Simonside, South Shields, Ty...

A Precautions
– I wouldn't use these tablets if you're allergic to them. You might come out in spots!
– And another thing – don't eat them, unless you want to sterilise your insides.
– Watch out that the kids don't get hold of them either.
– Oh and if you start feeling sick or anything, get down to your doctor's pdq.

B Nag Hammadi
At Nag Hammadi (funny old name, that) which is ooh, about 40km, no maybe 50, from Abydos, the Nile turns left a bit and rockets off to the Qena bend where the railway and road cross over to the other side. Nag Hammadi is a bit on the rural side – loads of cows, hens and stuff like that. Not a lot apart from that, so don't hang around too long here unless you're into farms, that is.

C Barton Fink (15)
This bloke who writes plays goes and stays in this hotel in Hollywood 'cos he needs the cash. It's a bit of a dump but anyway, he meets up with this fat weirdo in the next room who turns out to be a nutter who goes round killing people. Got it so far? Well, anyway, the writer gets this script to write and ...

G Put the helmet on and then shake your head to the left and to the right, foward and back, or try to turn the helmet with your hands. If it slips in any direction easily, the size is not the correct one for you.

Fits just right

H Dear Paul, I'm on a 3 month sabbatical ...sibly teaching but due to ...problems here am ...ing round. Spe... ...in Rajasthan ... ...Camel Fair ... ...azing photos (1 h... ...no of animal ther... ...g eunochs, false-... ...men – the lot! Am... ...evening in the Hi... ...ing to do some tre... ...the jungle – hope t... ...tigers things. Sor... ...seeing you in sum... ...ing if home at C...

I 1 General description
The engines fitted to all the Moto Guzzi ... this manual are of similar configuration. The en... share many identical components. The en... mounted in line with the frame, so that the ... ...dddall major castings ...

J My name is Frank Bascombe. I am a sportswriter.
For the past fourteen years I have lived here at 19 Hoving Road, Haddam, New Jersey, in a large Tudor house bought when a boo... of short stories I wrote sold to a movie producer for a lot of mo... ...emed to set my wife and me and our three children—tw... ...rn yet—up for a good life.

56

4 Three of the texts are not authentic. Which ones? Check your answers to Exercises 3 and 4 in the Key.

5 Tick the features that helped you identify the texts that were not authentic.

☐ the print used ☐ the punctuation
☐ the vocabulary ☐ the layout
☐ the illustration ☐ the grammar

Now look at the authentic versions of the three fake texts in the Key.

6 Look at the texts in Exercise 3 again. Write the letters of the text types where these features are used.

1 Use of imperative verbs _____
2 Use of passive verbs _____
3 First person narrative _____
4 Abbreviations and grammatically incomplete sentences _____
5 Formal use of vocabulary _____
6 Use of short phrases containing dense information _____
7 Long complex sentences _____
8 Use of simple present tense _____
9 Use of impersonal constructions _____
10 Use of technical vocabulary _____

Check list
When you plan, write and check your written work, think about appropriacy.

According to the text type

- decide how long and complete the sentences should be.
- decide which verb tenses are appropriate.
- choose a formal or informal style.
- select vocabulary carefully.
- observe layout conventions.

Extensive reading

These extensive reading texts are for your enjoyment rather than for intensive study. Try to avoid using a dictionary while you read. There is an optional exercise at the end.

This story, *The New Café*, is by Doris Lessing.

The New Café

There is a new café in our main street, Stephanie's, a year old now, and always full. It is French, like the 'Boucherie' next to it – a very British butcher – like the 'Brasserie' opposite, and it is run by two Greeks. At once it acquired its regulars, of whom I am one. Here, as in all good cafés, may be observed real-life soap operas, to be defined as series of emotional events that are certainly not unfamiliar, since you are bound to have seen something like them before, but to which you lack the key that will make them not trite, but shockingly individual.

The miraculous summer of 1989, when one hot blue day followed another, made pavement life as intense as in Paris or Rome, and our café had tables outside crammed against the aromatic offerings of a greengrocer. There everyone prefers to sit, but you are lucky to find a seat. Early in the summer two German girls appeared, large, attractive, uninhibitedly in search of boyfriends for their holidays. They were always together, usually outside, and for a few days sat alone eating the delicious cakes – genuinely French – that none can resist. They were delighted when someone – anyone – said, 'Is this chair free?' Once this was me. They had three weeks in London. They were in a small hotel ten minutes away. They thought London was a fine place. The weather was wonderful and – look! – how brown we are getting. While we chatted their eyes at once flew to anyone coming in.

And then they were with a young man. I had seen him here before. He sometimes dropped in for a coffee and was off at once. The German girls liked him. They leaned forward on their large and confident behinds and laughed and flung back blonde manes and all their rows of dewy teeth shone out at everybody. For they continued to keep an eye on possibilities. He leaned back in his chair, and entertained them. 'I like that one,' you could imagine one girl saying to another. 'He is a joker, I think?'

He was a likeable man, perhaps twenty-seven or eight, blue-eyed, fair haired – all that kind of thing, but he had

Unit 10

about him something that said, Keep Off. He was a little like a young hawk that hasn't yet got the hang of it, with a fluffy apprentice fierceness. And he was restless, always hooking and unhooking his legs, or flinging them hastily to one side to get them out of the way of someone coming past, or who seemed to sit too close.

For a few days the three of them were together, usually in the early afternoon. When they left, a girl was on either side of him. But there ought to be a fourth, and soon there he was. When the four met, inside the café or on the pavement, it did not seem as if they had paired off. The girls still kept their eyes on the entertainer, their bright mouths smiling in anticipation for the moment they could laugh, for that is what they liked best to do. And he sat watching them laugh, pleased he was giving them what they wanted, and the other young man, who did not seem to hope for much, laughed too.

Once or twice they ate a proper meal. Sometimes they talked about a film they had seen. One afternoon he came in with a dark composed girl who had a sisterly and satiric air. He bought her coffee and cakes and seemed apologetic about something. When the German girls came in he waved to them, tucked away his legs like an awkward parcel to make room, and the three girls and the man stayed for a time, and then went off together. Thereafter I saw him with the dark girl and with other girls and he treated them as he did the German girls, for he seemed to like them all.

Once two tables outside were empty and I sat at one and soon he was at the other, dropping into a chair at the last moment as he went past, as if he might as well do that as anything else. By now we were café acquaintances. He remarked that the summer wasn't bad at all and he was glad he hadn't gone to Spain, for it was better here. There was a week left of his holiday. He worked at the builders' supply shop down the road. It wasn't bad, he quite liked it. Sitting close to him in the strong light it could be seen that he was older than he seemed. There were lines under his eyes, and he was often abstracted, as if he were continually being removed from present surroundings by an inner buzzer: attend to this.

The German girls arrived and they were laughing in anticipation before they sat down.

Then they were not coming to the café, and he was back at work. He dropped in once or twice with a colleague from work, two young men wearing very white boiler suits, which were to make them look knowledgeable about building materials. The German girls' young man seemed frail inside the thick suit.

One day I was standing outside the Underground station, waiting to meet someone. He strolled past, taking his time, preoccupied. Then his face spread in a smile so unlike anything I had seen there, I quickly turned. Just ahead of him on the pavement was a young girl with a pram. No, when you looked she was a small pale young woman, probably twenty, and she was the baby's mother, from the tender way she bent to tuck it into already overwhelming covers. She smiled at the concealed baby, and then turned, startled, as the man came up and said in his whimsical, don't-take-me-seriously way, 'Hilda, it's me.' The two stood, dissolved in smiles. In a moment they would be in an embrace, but she recovered herself and quickly stood back. Then he, too, put on responsibility, as if fitting a winter's coat over his white boiler suit. Because he could not, apparently, embrace the mother, he leaned over the pram with a gallant air, and she leaned past him, lifted a bundle from its depths, and held the baby so that he could see its face. He bent politely over it and made appropriate noises, laughing at himself so that she had to laugh too. But all the time his eyes were on the young mother. She laughed again and pretended to thrust the baby at him for him to hold. At which he staggered back in a pantomime of an embarrassed male, and she fussed the bundle back under its covers and stood soberly, confronting him. He too was serious. They stood there a long time, long at least for an observer, perhaps a minute or more, looking at each other, entranced. These two were a match, a fit, the same kind: you had to say about them as you do, rarely, say about a couple: they are two halves of a whole, they belong together.

Again it was she who recovered herself and pushed the pram away down the pavement. Slowly pushed. After a few steps she turned to look at him. On she went – but turned again. He still stood there, gazing after her. She gave him a brave little wave, and went on. Slower, slower ... but she had to go on, she had to, and she reached the corner much too soon, where she stopped and looked back to where he stood, his face as miserable as hers. Again the seconds sped past ... But at last she firmly pushed the pram on and away and disappeared. Never has there been a corner of a street as empty as that one. He stared. She had gone. He took two steps to go after her, then came back, sending over his shoulder a quick glance: yes, she really had gone.

Slowly he walked on, slower, and stopped. He was level with me. He wasn't seeing anybody or anything, he was inside himself. He stood with his knees slightly bent, his arms loose, palms showing, his head back, as if he planned at some point to raise his eyes to the sky.

On the face of the charmed man chased emotions. There was regret, but a self-consciously dandyish regret, for even in his extremity he was not going to let go of this lifeline. There was bewilderment. There was loss. Above all, tenderness, banishing the others. Meanwhile his forehead was tense and his eyes sombre. What was he thinking? 'What was all that? What? But what happened ... what *did* happen, I don't understand what happened ... I don't understand ...'
Something like that.

7 Optional exercise. What was the young man's relationship with the girl he met at the end of the story? What is the reason for his sadness?

Unit 11

Vocabulary development — books

1 Find the odd word out in each group and explain your choice.

1 textbook comedy thriller	2 manual fable atlas	3 hilarious intriguing witty	4 saga poem fable
5 biography textbook short story	6 bold profound deep	7 leaf through plod through skip through	8 inane crass plodding

Vocabulary building — adjectives ending in *-ous*

Adjectives ending in *-ous* are used to describe someone or something as having a particular quality, for example *hilarious* and *riotous*.

Spelling note: there are a number of variations on the spelling of *-ous*, including the common ones *-eous*, *-ious* and *-uous*.

2 Form adjectives ending in *-ous* from these words:

ambiguity _____ caution _____

courage _____ curiosity _____

fame _____ mystery _____

religion _____ spontaneity _____

3 Now use the adjectives you have formed to complete these sentences:

1 He had been _____ in battle, so they gave him a medal.

2 I waved and the applause grew, a _____ display of friendship and affection.

3 Their grandson died of a _____ illness.

4 The collapse of Britain's most _____ company shocked the entire country.

5 There was nothing _____ in the message thumped out in his newspaper articles.

6 My sister and I were _____ children and delighted in finding out all sorts of things.

7 She could not accept the _____ beliefs of her parents.

8 Her husband is reserved and _____ , never making a swift decision about anything.

"Look out! It's a vicious circle!"

Unit 11

Listening

And then he kissed her ...

Mills and Boon is one of the biggest publishers of romantic fiction in the world. You are going to hear an extract from their cassette, *A Mills and Boon Guide to Writing Romantic Fiction*. In the extract advice is given about choosing a background for a story.

4 [S26] Listen and tick the backgrounds which are mentioned.

- [ ] a supermarket in London
- [ ] a language school in Brighton
- [ ] a hairdresser's in Edinburgh
- [ ] an international holiday resort
- [ ] a logging camp
- [ ] a woollen mill in Yorkshire
- [ ] a lawyer's office in London
- [ ] a sheep station in New Zealand
- [ ] a police station in Birmingham
- [ ] a factory in England

5 [S26] Read the statements below carefully. Listen again and decide which statements are true and which are false.

1. [ ] The narrator says sophisticated settings are more popular than others.
2. [ ] Settings which seem attractive to some people seem boring for others.
3. [ ] Readers have written to Mills and Boon asking for specific settings for stories.
4. [ ] The most important thing about any setting is that the details should be accurate.
5. [ ] You shouldn't set your story in an office because lots of readers are secretaries.
6. [ ] Mills and Boon didn't publish the story *Tigers on his Track* because it was set in Australia.
7. [ ] The book set in Venice was rejected because of factual mistakes.

Pronunciation — weak forms - auxiliary verbs

6 [S27] Listen to these sentences from *And then he kissed her...* Decide if the auxiliary verbs are used in their strong or weak form. Write *S* for strong or *W* for weak.

1. had [ ]
2. was [ ]
   were [ ]
3. would [ ]
4. are [ ]
   is [ ]
5. have [ ]
6. may [ ]
7. can [ ]
8. would [ ]

Check your answers in the Key.

Reading

7 Read these three sentences summarising the point of view expressed in the article. Read the article and choose the most appropriate summary.

A ☐ Romantic fiction should be taken more seriously because it is great literature. It receives little attention from reviewers because it sells so well.

B ☐ There is a long tradition of romantic fiction in British literature but this genre is largely ignored by reviewers or is not taken seriously.

C ☐ It is time to take romantic fiction more seriously because men have started writing it.

Obsession, love, betrayal, intrigue - these are themes with which the novel has always concerned itself. Despite changing fashions in literature and social mores, the basic elements have remained the same. A love story, however much it is camouflaged with high-flown language or post-modern trickery, remains a love story: a variation on the theme of boy-meets-girl.

Consider the following scenarios: an independent young woman falls in love with her employer, winning his love through sheer force of personality despite the more flamboyant attractions of her rival; an intelligent, attractive heroine is drawn in spite of herself to a rich but heartless man who thinks himself too good for her; and a headstrong young woman running her own business learns the value of a long-standing relationship only after she had been disastrously involved with a number of unsuitable men.

These are not the plots of contemporary mass market fiction but those of novels which were, in their own day, as popular in their appeal. They are, respectively, the plots of Charlotte Brontë's *Jane Eyre*, Jane Austen's *Pride and Prejudice* and Thomas Hardy's *Far from the Madding Crowd* - novels which no-one would be foolish enough to dismiss as trivial merely because they deal with universal themes. Yet imagine the critical reception Emily Brontë's *Wuthering Heights*, with its period setting, star-crossed lovers and elemental passions, would receive today. 'Blockbuster' and 'bodice-ripper' are some of the kinder epithets a reviewer might use - if such a book were reviewed at all.

For, despite the wide readership enjoyed by contemporary romantic fiction, it receives little or no attention in the review pages of newspapers and magazines, in which even the most mediocre 'literary' novel can be sure of a few column inches. The reason given for this is generally that romance (from the relatively anonymous works published by Mills & Boon to works by highly successful and established authors such as Maeve Binchy and Catherine Cookson) doesn't 'need' reviewing, because it already sells so well. Needless to say, this argument is never used to limit the space given to crime fiction or any other male-dominated genre.

'If popular fiction is reviewed, it is always tongue-in-cheek,' says Sue Fletcher, editorial fiction director and joint deputy managing director of Headline book publishers. 'It's a snobbish attitude which is, regrettably, endemic in the publishing business.'

Jill Black of the Romantic Novelists' Association also believes that things are now changing for the better. 'Romantic fiction has opened out into a much bigger concern, dealing with a whole range of experience. Perhaps because we now have a number of male writers entering the field, romance is being treated with a great deal more respect, compared with the days when it was regarded as very much a "women's interest" and therefore something to be patronised.' Certainly, the success of a novel such as A S Byatt's Booker prize-winning *Possession* (subtitled *A Romance*), which blends erudite literary allusion with a tale of clandestine Victorian passion, would seem to substantiate this view. Byatt's novel is not the only one to offer this combination of academic background and romantic theme. David Lodge attempted something similar in *Small World*, in which a handsome young research student specialising in medieval romance pursues an elusive beauty halfway around the globe before he can declare his love. In its fusion of contemporary romance and courtly love, Lodge's novel links present-day forms of romantic fiction with their precursors in the medieval *chansons*. Regarded in this light, the traditional Mills & Boon romance is only a popular reworking of an earlier and highly sophisticated literary form.

Like its medieval forerunner, even Mills & Boon has changed with the times. The stereotypical images its novels once projected have given way to more realistic concerns. Luigi Bonomi, senior editor at Mills & Boon, says, 'Increasingly, our authors are reflecting the changing role of women in society - dealing with issues such as adultery, abortion, and the conflicting demands of career and family life.' Despite this shift of emphasis, the stereotypical image of romantic fiction remains - and with it the sneering attitude of the literary establishment. Bonomi takes the view that romantic fiction is seen as of no importance just because it is written and read by women.

So what makes a really great romance? Lisa Appignanesi, an academic who also writes romantic fiction, thinks that there is no easy formula. 'It's something to do with the narrative drive which compels the reader to go on. And of course the characters have to be good.' Writers of popular fiction, she argues, are working within a tradition which goes back to that of the 19th-century realist novel. 'With the romance, you're dealing with the traditional feminine domain of the emotions - with love and caring, desire and sexuality. These are themes which, once you let them in, tend to dominate a book. Kurt Vonnegut once remarked that his novels don't deal with love because "love takes over" once you start to write about it.' ■

Unit 11

8 Read these topic sentences carefully. Read the article again. Write the number of the paragraph which each sentence relates to.

A ☐ An account of the changes in content of Mills and Boon novels.

B ☐ The view that literary reviewers are dismissive of romantic fiction.

C ☐ A list of the main ingredients of a love story.

D ☐ The titles of some 'respectable' love stories which are considered landmarks of English literature.

E ☐ The view that the characteristic common to good romantic novels is a strong narrative which makes the reader want to keep reading.

F ☐ A theory about why romantic fiction is now being taken a bit more seriously.

G ☐ The plots of two famous love stories.

H ☐ Reasons for romantic fiction being ignored by reviewers.

Phrasal verbs — *give way (to)*

> In the article about romantic fiction the phrasal verb *give way (to)* is used in the sentence *The stereotypical images its novels once projected have given way to more realistic concerns* meaning 'have been replaced by'.

Look at these five meanings of *give way (to)*.

1. (with *to*) be replaced by
2. collapse
3. (with *to*) agree to allow someone to do something even though you disapprove
4. (with *to*) allow yourself to show an emotion or something you feel strongly about, especially by losing control
5. slow down or stop when driving a car in order to allow another car or vehicle to pass

9 Match the context sentences below to the five meanings of *give way (to)*.

A ☐ In the end it was easier to give way to his requests, even though we really didn't want to.

B ☐ The beautiful fields near the river where I played as a child were giving way to fashionable houses for the middle class people of the town.

C ☐ When you are approaching a roundabout you have to give way to cars approaching from your left.

D ☐ He was extremely annoyed at himself for giving way to tears at the end of the film.

E ☐ I wouldn't put that piano on the second floor - it weighs a ton and the floor might give way.

10 Now complete these sentences using a form of *give way (to)*.

1. The council really disagreed with the government's decision to build a by-pass but...

2. When I heard that our cat had been run over...

3. When you come up to a junction and there is a solid white line on the road...

4. Although the sky was full of grey thunder clouds in the morning, later in the day...

5. Thirty people who had been working on the second floor of the building were seriously injured when...

Idioms `tongue`

> In the article about romantic fiction the expression *tongue-in-cheek* is used in the sentence *If popular fiction is reviewed, it is always tongue-in-cheek*. The expression *tongue-in-cheek* means 'in an insincere way' or 'as a joke'.

11 Explain the meaning of the other phrases using *tongue* in these sentences.

1 When the police officer asked him his name and address, he became completely tongue-tied and just mumbled incoherently.
2 'She sells sea-shells on the sea shore' is one of the best known tongue-twisters in English.
3 Even though I was very angry with them I held my tongue and pretended nothing had happened.
4 The boy acted as if he had lost his tongue and we couldn't even find out where he lived.
5 He's Greek and I have great difficulty getting my tongue round his name, so I usually call him George.
6 I didn't mean to say that - it was just a slip of the tongue.

Grammar `comparisons`

12 Write sentences comparing these things. Use *more/less; as, like* and their submodifiers.

1 a weekend in Paris / a weekend in Manchester
2 Rottweiler dogs / poodles
3 married life / life as a single person
4 life imprisonment / the death penalty
5 family holidays / holidays alone
6 working for a company / working for yourself

Writing

13 On page 87 of your Student's Book you chose three books to take to a desert island. Write a short composition about your books. Mention these things:

- title and author
- anything interesting about the author
- a brief summary of the plot or content of each book
- your reason(s) for choosing it

Alternatively, write about one of the short stories that you have read in the Workbook.

Unit 12

Vocabulary development — education

1 Write a paragraph about the education system in your country. Mention these topics. Use words from page 93 of your Student's Book.

- types of school
- minimum leaving age
- teachers and qualifications
- discipline problems
- class size
- examinations

Vocabulary building — adjectives in -ive

> There are many adjectives ending in -ive, like *comprehensive* on page 93 of your Students' Book. Many are derived from stems which are no longer common in modern English, although this is not always the case. For example, *expensive* means 'costly' and is based on the stem *expense*.

2 Convert these words into adjectives ending in -ive.

imagine	attract	produce	protect
create	decide	conclude	offend

3 Now write a context sentence to demonstrate the meaning of the adjectives you have formed.

Reading

Some people feel that they were failed by the education system, and were pushed into the wrong job because they studied the wrong subjects and had to choose a direction too early in their school career.

4 Read this extract from the biography of a famous British musician. Can you guess who the musician is?

> 'I had failed the eleven-plus miserably,' says Eric. 'Then I qualified to take the thirteen-plus, which was something new they'd introduced. I passed that in art and English, and because my marks were good in those two subjects I was sent to Hollyfield Road School, which had an art branch. We did ordinary lessons like English, mathematics, woodwork and physical training some days, then there would be three or four solid days of art alone. We worked with clay and paint and did still-lifes and figure drawing, and we also had the bonus of going to Kingston Art School night classes.
> 'When I was sixteen, at Hollyfield, I took my GCE O levels and got an A in art and an O in English. This didn't really qualify me for anything.' But he was building up an enthusiasm for a career in art.
> 'So I took a portfolio to Kingston. I didn't have enough certificates, but they liked what they saw. They did an interview to get me in and I got into the art school for one year on probation. Students go for four years, and in that first year they weigh you up. And at the end of the first year, simply because of my lack of interest and a lot of distractions (at that point I was sixteen, getting into the Bohemian, beatnik thing and listening to music and not really working very much), I didn't have a big enough portfolio for them to think it was worth keeping me on. The stuff I did was good. But there just wasn't enough - they were judging by quantity. So I didn't make it. They booted me out, along with another bloke - us two out of fifty, which wasn't too good.'
> There had been an unfortunate start to his entry to art school. 'When they had asked which side of the college I wanted to go in, Fine Art or Graphics, I said Graphics. I'd been slightly brainwashed by Rose and Jack that if you wanted to make a living in art, you had to be a commercial artist. And I was nodding my head to that at the interview. They said: "What do you want to be?" I said, "Commercial artist." So they put me into Graphics. And after the first couple of weeks in Graphics, I realized that I was in the wrong department, because in the canteen I saw all the good blokes with paint all over them and long hair, and they were in the Fine Art department! And all our lot looked like chartered accountants! So I really thought I'd blown it from the word go. I just then started getting more interested in playing the guitar and listening to music.'

Unit 12

5 Multiple matching

Read the extract again carefully. Match the descriptions on the left with the information on the right.

1	Exams that used to be taken in England at the age of sixteen.	a	Hollyfield Road School
2	The names of the people who looked after the protagonist as a boy.	b	Kingston Art School
3	The name of the school he attended at the age of thirteen.	c	Eleven-plus
4	The branch of art which he was encouraged to study.	d	O-levels
5	The place where he studied art full-time.	e	Rose and Jack
6	An exam taken at the age of eleven which decided the type of school you went to.	f	Graphics

Idioms `blow`

> In the extract about a famous musician the verb *blow* is used in the sentence *So I really thought I'd blown it from the word go*. This idiomatic use of *blow* means 'to fail to take full advantage of an opportunity.'

6 Choose the correct meaning for these uses of *blow* in idiomatic expressions.

1 It's rumoured that MI5's intelligence network in East Germany was **blown** when the Berlin Wall came down.

   a exposed ☐   b exploded ☐   c investigated ☐

2 We **blew** fifty pounds each on drinks at an Argentinian tango club in Paris.

   a were cheated of ☐   b wasted ☐   c spent ☐

3 Enjoy yourself while you can and **blow** what happens tomorrow.

   a worry about ☐   b don't worry about ☐
   c concentrate on ☐

4 *Zen and the Art of Motorcycle Maintenance* really **blew my mind** when I first read it.

   a excited me ☐   b was unintelligible to me ☐
   c made me angry ☐

Phrasal verbs `keep`

In the extract the phrasal verb *keep on* is used in the sentence *I didn't have a big enough portfolio for them to think it was worth keeping me on*. Here *keep on* means 'to continue to allow to stay'.

7 The verb *keep* is used with many other particles as a phrasal verb. Circle the correct particle in these sentences.

1 We are trying to keep costs **down/up** so that we don't discourage first-time buyers.

2 There have been a lot of thefts from our local builder's yard so the owners have bought an Alsation dog in an effort to keep people **out of/in** the yard when they are not there.

3 She's such a fast runner that I had great difficulty keeping **up/down** with her.

4 The teacher kept her class **out/in** after school because they had behaved so badly on the school trip to the Houses of Parliament.

5 The children have eaten most of the food, I'm afraid. But I've kept **in/back** some ice-cream for you.

6 I found the exercise rather difficult but I kept **on/at** it and finished at one in the morning.

7 Her parents tried to keep her **at/from** going to the party but she just climbed out of her bedroom window and went anyway.

8 The editor kept **to/in** her schedule and the book came out on time.

Unit 12

Listening

8 [S28] You are going to hear an Italian teacher, Maria Vittoria Maulini, talking about her education. Read the questions below carefully. Listen and answer.

1 Which part of her education did Maria Vittoria enjoy most and why?
2 How did things change when she went on to secondary education?
3 How did the particular period affect Maria Vittoria's time at *Liceo*?
4 What is Maria Vittoria's main criticism of her teachers?
5 What was good about her course at university?
6 What has her education left her with?
7 How is education different now according to Maria Vittoria?

Pronunciation — elision - vowels before *n*

9 [S29] Listen to these sentences. Underline the words in bold if the vowels /ə/ or /ɪ/ are elided.

1 What was **certain** was that this had been the worst recession since the War.
2 I can't see the **difference** between studying English at school and studying it in **England**.
3 **Patience** is one of the most useful qualities in a language teacher.
4 Alternative **medicine** has become very popular in **Britain** over the last few years.
5 It might be **prudent** to book tickets for the train as it's a Bank Holiday.
6 We have had **correspondence** with the owners of the supermarket and we are now waiting for a **decision**.

Grammar — reported speech

Read this conversation from the novel *A Slipping-Down Life* by the American writer, Anne Tyler.

'Who's this?' Evie asked.
'It's Drumstrings Casey, who do you think?'
'Do you know him?'
'No. Do you think it's a good likeness?'
'Oh, well, sure,' said Evie. 'But how were you - did you ask him to sit for it?'
'No, I did it at the Unicorn. That's where he plays, same as Joseph Ballew. Joseph Ballew is my real favourite, but I think this one is kind of cute too. You ever been to the Unicorn?'
'I don't even know what it is,' Evie said.
'It's a roadhouse. Just south of Pulqua a ways. You can come with me sometime, I got a car I can borrow.'
'Tomorrow?'
'What?'
'Are you going there tomorrow?'
'Tomorrow's Friday. Casey only plays on Saturdays.'
'Will you be going there this Saturday?'
'Sure, I guess so.'
'I'll come with you then,' Evie said. 'Could I bring a friend?'
'Sure. And keep the picture, if you like.'
'Well, thank you, I don't have anything to trade for it.'
'To-?'
'Trade. Trade for the picture.'
'Why would you want to trade for it?'
'I don't know,' Evie said.

10 Write a summary of the conversation. Remember that when you are reporting dialogue, you don't have to use the speakers' exact words. Use a variety of reporting verbs.

Writing — formal letters

11 Imagine that you have decided to apply for a place on an Open University course to study English literature.

Write a letter of application containing the following information:

- your age
- your educational background
- your reasons for applying
- request for more information about the course, including starting date, cost, timetable

Lay out your letter properly. Use the correct language for the opening and closing salutations. Put your address and the University's address in the right places.
The address of the Open University is
Open University, Wood Lane, Shepherd's Bush, London SW1.

Unit 12

Extension and consolidation

Editing

1 There are fifteen deliberate punctuation mistakes in this extract from *Summerhill* by A. S. Neill. Correct the mistakes.

In the home, the child is always being taught. In almost every home, there is always at least, one ungrown-up grownup who rushes to show Tommy how his engine works There is always someone to lift the baby up on a chair when baby wants to examine something on the wall: Every time we show Tommy how his engine work's we are stealing from that child the joy of life - the joy of discovery - the joy of overcoming an obstacle. Worse? We make that child come to believe that he is inferior; and must depend on help.

Parents, are slow in realizing how unimportant the learning side of school is. children like adults learn what they want to learn. All prize-giving and marks and exams sidetrack proper personality development? Only pedants claim that learning from books is education,

Dictation

2 Read this extract from the article by Lucy Ellmann on page 89 of your Students' Book. Try to fill in the gaps. Use a pencil.

This Friday, the Irish president _____ present American author Norman Rush _____ the *Irish Times*-Aer Lingus International _____ Prize (a cool twenty-five thousand _____) for his novel, *Mating*. I _____ one of the five judges, _____ involved flying First Class to Dublin _____ times, eating at expensive restaurants _____ - the down side - reading forty-six _____ . Normally it would take me _____ least four years to read _____ books. Not only that, but the discussion meetings we were _____ upon to give little speeches, _____ the cuff, on our favourites _____ rejects. I am no orator; everything _____ say needs rewrites. The fee _____ a lure, but a friend _____ that at the rate I _____ reading I was being paid _____ twenty pence an hour.

3 [S30] Now listen to a recording of the extract. Complete the extract with the original words.

Extensive reading

These extensive reading exercises are for your enjoyment rather than for intensive study. Try to avoid using a dictionary while you read. There is an optional exercise at the end.

This is a chapter from the first part of *Boy*, the autobiography of Roald Dahl.

First day

In September 1925, when I was just nine, I set out on the first great adventure of my life - boarding-school. My mother had chosen for me a Prep School in a part of England which was as near as it could possibly be to our home in South Wales, and it was called St Peter's. The full postal address was St Peter's School, Weston-super-Mare, Somerset.

Weston-super-Mare is a slightly seedy seaside resort with a vast sandy beach, a tremendous long pier, an esplanade running along the sea-front, a clutter of hotels and boarding-houses, and about ten thousand little shops selling buckets and spades and sticks of rock and ice-creams. It lies almost directly across the Bristol Channel from Cardiff, and on a clear day you can stand on the esplanade at Weston and look across the fifteen or so miles of water and see the coast of Wales lying pale and milky on the horizon.

In those days the easiest way to travel from Cardiff to Weston-super-Mare was by boat. Those boats were beautiful. They were paddle-steamers, with gigantic swishing paddle-wheels on their flanks, and the wheels made the most terrific noise as they sloshed and churned through the water.

On the first day of my first term I set out by taxi in the afternoon with my mother to catch the paddle-steamer from Cardiff Docks to Weston-super-Mare. Every piece of clothing I wore was brand new and had my name on it. I wore black shoes, grey woollen stockings with blue turnovers, grey flannel shorts, a grey shirt, a red tie, a grey flannel blazer with the blue school crest on the breast pocket and a grey school cap with the same crest just above the peak. Into the taxi that was taking us to the docks went my brand new trunk and my brand new tuck-box, and both had R. DAHL painted on them in black.

A tuck-box is a small pinewood trunk which is very strongly made, and no boy has ever gone as a boarder to an English Prep School without one. It is his own secret store-house, as secret as a lady's handbag, and there is an unwritten law that no other boy, no teacher, not even the Headmaster himself has the right to pry into the contents of your tuck-box. The owner has the key in his pocket and that is where it stays. At St Peter's, the tuck-boxes were ranged shoulder to shoulder all around the four walls of the changing-room and your own tuck-box stood directly below the peg on which you hung your games clothes. A tuck-box, as the name implies, is a box in which you store your tuck. At Prep School in those days, a parcel of tuck was sent once a week by anxious mothers to their ravenous little sons, and an average tuck-box would probably contain, at almost any time, half a home-made currant cake, a packet of squashed-fly biscuits, a couple of oranges, an apple, a banana, a pot of strawberry jam or Marmite, a bar of chocolate, a bag of Liquorice Allsorts and a tin of Bassett's lemonade powder. An English school in those days was purely a money-making business owned and operated by the Headmaster. It suited him, therefore, to give the boys as little food as possible himself and to encourage the parents in various cunning ways to feed their offspring by parcel-post from home.

'By all means, my dear Mrs Dahl, *do* send your boy some little treats now and again,' he would say. 'Perhaps a few oranges and apples once a week' - fruit was very expensive - 'and a nice currant cake, a *large* currant cake perhaps because small boys have large appetites do they not, ha-ha-ha...Yes, yes, as *often* as you like. *More* than once a week if you wish ... *Of course* he'll be getting plenty of good food here, the best there is, but it never tastes *quite* the same as home cooking, does it? I'm sure you wouldn't want him to be the only one who doesn't get a lovely parcel from home every week.'

As well as tuck, a tuck-box would also contain all manner of treasures such as a magnet, a pocket-knife, a compass, a ball of string, a clockwork racing-car, half a dozen lead soldiers, a box of conjuring-tricks, some tiddly-winks, a Mexican jumping bean, a catapult, some foreign stamps, a couple of stink-bombs, and I remember one boy called Arkle who drilled an airhole in the lid of his tuck-box and kept a pet frog in there which he fed on slugs.

So off we set, my mother and I and my trunk and my tuck-box, and we boarded the paddle-steamer and went swooshing across the Bristol Channel in a shower of spray. I liked that part of it, but I began to grow apprehensive as I disembarked on to the pier at Weston-super-Mare and watched my trunk and tuck-box being loaded into an English taxi which would drive us to St Peter's. I had absolutely no idea what was in store for me. I had never spent a single night away from our large family before.

St Peter's was on a hill above the town. It was a long three-storeyed stone building that looked rather like a private lunatic asylum, and in front of it lay the playing-fields with their three football pitches. One-third of the building was reserved for the Headmaster and his family. The rest of it housed the boys, about one hundred and fifty of them altogether, if I remember rightly.

As we got out of the taxi, I saw the whole driveway abustle with small boys and their parents and their trunks and their tuck-boxes, and a man I took to be the Headmaster was swimming around among them shaking everybody by the hand.

I have already told you that *all* Headmasters are giants, and this one was no exception. He advanced upon my mother and shook her by the hand, then he shook me by the hand and as he did so he gave me the kind of flashing grin a shark might give to a small fish just before he gobbles it up. One of his front teeth, I noticed, was edged all the way round with gold, and his hair was slicked down with so much hair-cream that it glistened like butter.

'Right,' he said to me. 'Off you go and report to the Matron.' And to my mother he said briskly, 'Goodbye, Mrs Dahl. I shouldn't linger if I were you. We'll look after him.'

My mother got the message. She kissed me on the cheek and said goodbye and climbed right back into the taxi.

The Headmaster moved away to another group and I was left standing there beside my brand new trunk and my brand new tuck-box. I began to cry.

4 **Optional exercise.** What information do you find out about starting school in England in the 20s and how is it different from when you went to school? Write a paragraph summarising what you have concluded.

Unit 13

Vocabulary development — television and film

1 Write a review of a film you have seen recently either at the cinema or on television. Use the answers to these questions as a framework for your review.

What is the title of the film?
Who is the director?
Who are the main actors or actresses?
Where and when was the film made?
What genre does it belong to?
What is the mood of the film?
What are the performances of the leading actors or actresses like?

Vocabulary building — adjectives ending in -ic

-ic combines with nouns to form adjectives, for example, *atmosphere* + *-ic* makes *atmospheric*. Adjectives formed in this way describe something as resembling, involving or being connected with the thing referred to by the original noun. For example, *atmospheric* music has a lot of atmosphere.
-ic also combines with nouns ending in *-ist* that refer to people. For example, if someone is *optimistic*, they have a lot of *optimism* about the future.

2 Form adjectives ending in *-ic* from these nouns.

alcohol _____
nationalist _____
photograph _____
democrat _____
artist _____
moralist _____
enthusiast _____
pessimist _____
irony _____
poet _____

3 Now write a sentence for each adjective you have formed to show its meaning.

Phrasal verbs — put up

In the listening text on page 98 of your Students' Book the phrase *And because the television companies put up the money...* is used. The phrasal verb *put up* here means 'provide'.

Look at these nine meanings of *put up*.

1 move to a higher position
2 push something up into another thing
3 build or fix in place
4 open or spread out something which is folded
5 oppose, resist or fight
6 suggest for discussion
7 raise the cost of
8 give accommodation to
9 choose to be a candidate

4 Use the skeletons to write a context sentence for each of the nine meanings of *put up*. Write them in the same order as the definitions above.

umbrella - raining

proposal - meeting

government - price of beer

painting - wall

fight - World Boxing Championship

her party - election

brush - chimney - clean

collar - jacket

my flat - three days

Unit 13

Idioms eye

In the listening text on page 98 of your Students' Book two idioms with the word *eye* are used.
In *Do you think that film directors have one eye on video when they produce films these days*, *have one eye on* means 'secretly or discreetly paying attention to'.
In *They're shooting more for television as opposed to cinema and they don't have that eye*, *have (that) eye* means 'recognise clearly and make good judgements'.

5 Work out what these idiomatic expressions mean from the context. Write a definition for each sentence.

1 The children were all eyes at the circus.
2 He ran his eye over the newspaper article.
3 Can you catch the waiter's eye?
4 I've had my eye on you for a long time.
5 Keep your eyes peeled for pickpockets on Oxford Street.
6 Can you keep an eye on the baby while I go shopping?
7 He was making eyes at the waitress.
8 I thought the matter was quite straightforward but now I realise there's more to it than meets the eye.
9 She doesn't see eye to eye with her parents.
10 Sal is still up to her eyes in kids and shopping.

Pronunciation word boundary assimilation

On page 98 of your Students' Book you studied the way the sounds /d/, /n/, /s/, /t/ and /z/ combine with certain following consonants to produce new sounds.

6 How are these words and phrases pronounced?

1 Look at that page   She'd better come
  She's in Paris

2 The first year   I've found you at last

3 Students showed their work   In case you get there late
  Here's your lunch   He was shown to his room

4 Not quite   He would get there late
  She was thrown clear   They won't get a rise

[S31] Now listen and check your pronunciation.

Listening

7 [S32] Listen to Paul talking about how he came to love the cinema. Answer the questions.

1 Make notes of what he says about these cinemas:

  The Ritz   The Gaumont   The Odeon   The Conway
  The Cambrian   The Celtic

2 What is the significance of these films for Paul?

  The Comancheros   *Pipe-Laying in Siberia*   *Ben Hur*

3 Where did he work as a student and how did this help to develop his passion for the cinema?

4 What happened during the showing of *Ben Hur* which he mentions?

70

Unit 13

Reading

8 Read this article about a film lover and his very own cinema. Choose the best phrase for each space. Write the number next to the phrase.

Home movies

Don Parr spent his life in films ____1____ as a projectionist at the Apollo in north Birmingham, until it was demolished to make way for a shopping centre. Then he went on the road after work, showing films in social clubs ____2____ toolmaking, to be manager of a cinema in Solihull until that, too, closed, the victim of an eight-screener that had opened round the corner. ____3____ with his wife and his dog. But he did not want to sever all links with the love of his life. So, in an age of multiplexes, Don built his own cinema. In a shed at the bottom of his garden, ____4____ which is a copy of the old Apollo in Erdington, right down to a plaque above the screen of Apollo in his godly chariot. It has a grand proscenium arch. It has a curtain that swishes electrically open and closed. ____5____ just like a proper picture house. It has tip-up seats. It has heating and air conditioning. It has a board outside advertising forthcoming attractions. ____6____ is that it seats just 15 people. It cost Don £5,000 to build. ____7____ which meant that Don didn't need planning permission. Don and his neighbour, John, are the projectionists. Don likes to show musicals and cowboy films from the Thirties, Forties and Fifties. ____8____ he calls 'very violent films' such as *Terminator II*. 'We get enough of that on the telly.' He says his favourite film is *The Sound of Music* - an affection undimmed by having projected it hundreds of times.

____9____ the running order of the last night at the old Apollo from Saturday 2 April, 1960, with *Last Train From Gun Hill* and the national anthem at 10.22pm.

____10____ he first found as a teenager in wartime Birmingham when he saw Charlie Chaplin in *The Gold Rush*. 'I just like coming here,' he says, adjusting the screen for Cinemascope, 'and losing myself.'

A ☐ From the outside it looks like a garden shed...
B ☐ Don, 65, is preserving the escapism...
C ☐ Film buffs and friends gather at Don's cinema...
D ☐ First he worked part-time...
E ☐ It has Muzak as you go in...
F ☐ At the entrance to the Apollo is...
G ☐ He will not show what...
H ☐ So Don retired to his east Birmingham semi...
I ☐ Then he quit his job...
J ☐ The only difference from the real thing...

Unit 13

Grammar — participles

9 Modify or combine these sentences to include a participle.

Example: Shirley had forgotten her umbrella, so she took shelter from the rain in the library.

Having forgotten her umbrella, Shirley took shelter from the rain in the library.

1 I sat in the living room and read a book until our friends arrived.
2 As they are fluent in three languages, Betty and her husband are often invited to parties at the embassy.
3 When we were in Milan last week we saw many children who were begging in the streets.
4 After she had put the car in the garage, Wendy went into the house.
5 The bell rang and when I opened the door there was a group of children who were singing.
6 On Thursday my sister turned up at my house. She was wearing a bright red evening dress.
7 Because I had lost my ticket, I had to pay again when the inspector came round.
8 We arrived at the airport two hours before the flight so we went and had lunch.

10 Now do either A or B.

A Write a letter to the newspaper in reply, commenting on and agreeing or disagreeing with the views of this teacher.

B Write a composition of 250-300 words on the topic, 'Violence on television has a negative effect on children.'

Writing

Read this letter to the *Independent* newspaper about violence on television.

To see the influence of TV violence, visit a playground

AS A TEACHER, I come across many children from happy homes who have television in their bedrooms and watch until closedown ('Keep violence off our screens, says Major', 7 March).

These children watch an unadulterated diet of violence, sex, rape and torture, and the next morning act it out in the playground. If Alan Yentob doesn't believe in the direct imitative response to violence, he should watch children miming the actions of the previous night's horrors. 'We're only playing,' they happily protest, and indeed they are. But all play is merely preparation for adulthood. Today's generation has been well 'prepared' and we are now reaping the results. It is naïve and hypocritical to imagine that children watching television night after night will be influenced by the adverts for sweets and toys but unaffected by continual depravity.

Children learn by example, and cannot often distinguish between fact and fantasy, between reality and television. Television comes into our homes and should be fit for family viewing at all times. Maybe there should be a watchdog committee similar to those for water, gas and electricity, made up of ordinary viewers.

Television has more power than Parliament and it is abusing that power. It must be restrained.

E Jenkins
Liverpool

Unit 14

Vocabulary development — art

1 Write a word for each of these definitions.

1 A drawing that is done quickly without a lot of details. _____

2 A painting which shows a scene in the countryside. _____

3 An extremely good painting. _____

4 A painting or drawing of an arrangement of inanimate objects such as flowers or fruit. _____

5 A style of art which uses shapes and patterns to represent things, people and ideas rather than showing people or things as they actually look. _____

6 A modern copy of a painting. _____

7 A painting of a person, often showing only the face. _____

8 A picture made with a pencil, pen or crayon which usually only shows the outlines of something. _____

9 The coloured liquid used for writing, drawing or printing. _____

2 Now use the same words to complete these sentences.

1 When you fill in official forms they usually ask you to write in _____ .

2 I find paintings by _____ artists like Jackson Pollock quite fascinating but I couldn't tell you what they were about.

3 When I was at the market on Saturday I found a good cheap _____ of the *Laughing Cavalier*.

4 In Florence there are many good pavement artists who will do a quick _____ of you for just a few pounds.

5 My sister gave me a very elaborate pen and ink _____ of Richmond Bridge.

6 Van Gogh's _____ *Sunflowers* is one of the world's most valuable paintings.

7 One of the most popular paintings in the Louvre is the _____ called the *Mona Lisa*.

8 Gainsborough is possibly the best known and loved _____ painter in Britain.

9 One of my favourite paintings is a _____ by Vermeer. It shows a bowl of fruit next to an earthenware jug.

Vocabulary building — words ending in *-side*

> Nouns and adjectives ending in *-side* fall into two categories:
> 1 The edge of something
> - *side* combines with nouns to form words that refer to the edge of the place or object in the original noun, for example, the *riverside* is an area on or near the bank of a river.
> 2 Part of something
> -*side* combines with nouns and adjectives to form words that refer to that part of something that involves or is described by the original noun or adjective.
> 3 Words with other meanings
> There is a third category of words that do not belong to either of these groups, for example, *countryside*.

3 Decide which category these words containing *-side* belong to.

aside ☐   reside ☐   seaside ☐
trackside ☐   alongside ☐   dockside ☐
lakeside ☐   passenger-side ☐   underside ☐
inside ☐   farside ☐   roadside ☐

Now add two more words to each category.

Pronunciation — weak vowels

4 [S33] Listen to these sentences and underline the words which contain this sound: /ə/.

1 In November there was the annual visit by the owner of the factory.

2 Actually she's not as introverted as she might seem at first.

3 We had a very romantic evening at a new restaurant in the centre of London.

4 She's a brilliant pianist who studied at the Conservatory in Paris.

5 Property is the most valuable asset during times of monetary instability.

Now listen and repeat. Concentrate on pronouncing the weak vowel accurately.

Unit 14

Listening

5 [S34] Henry Meryck-Hughes is the Director of the Hayward Gallery in London. Listen to what he says about his work at the Gallery and make notes under these headings.

- His three main responsibilities
- Current exhibitions at the Hayward Gallery
- Weak points of the Gallery
- Future plans for the Gallery

Reading

6 Read this text by a famous copyist, Tom Keating. Tick the names of the painters he has imitated. Be careful! He mentions some artists that he has not imitated.

> In the middle sixties when I began to emulate Goya and the other great masters, I often felt their spirits actually guiding my hands. Most people either don't believe me or think I'm round the bend when I tell them this. But it is terrifyingly true and to me not particularly surprising. After all, most people can feel the sense of power that radiates from a Rembrandt, Tintoretto, or El Greco and what other way is there to define that feeling than to say that the spirit of the master is living on in the very fibre of the canvas?
>
> One of the first times that I experienced this feeling was in 1962 when I was living in Kew. I was doodling in pastel on a sheet of Ingres paper, when suddenly I began to feel very tired. I lay down on my bed and as it got dark I got the strange feeling that I was floating. Then a feeling of oppression, of being pulled down. It felt so awful that I vomited and cried. I slept fitfully and seem to recall getting up several times during the night. When I woke up the next morning there on my easel was a self-portrait of Degas. I know that I must have done it, but I had no memory of it. The only Van Gogh that I ever painted happened in a similar way. I couldn't paint a Goya, Rembrandt or even a Samuel Palmer for a million pounds or to save my life. But when the spirit of a long-dead artist comes into my hands the images flow out on to the canvas without the slightest effort on my part. I am not a spiritualist and I have never dabbled in the occult; I cannot account for the strange thing that happens to me and will not try.
>
> Not all painters have 'come down' to me in this way, but those that have leave a stamp on the picture that is unmistakably their own - usually in the haunting quality of the eyes. They follow you round the room like those of the famous *Laughing Cavalier* in the Wallace Collection.
>
> As an extra precaution, to avoid experts mistaking my Sextons for the real thing, I sometimes wrote a swear word, 'ever been had' or 'this is a fake' directly on the canvas before starting work. I'm told that these messages, which were written in white lead paint, will show up under a picture if it is X-rayed.
>
> Another little dodge of mine was that before fixing the old brown paper to the back of a water-colour frame - with flour paste, never use modern glue or you're bound to come unstuck - I'd scrawl something like: 'Mr Palmer will call for this, Thursday 4 o'clock,' or, 'Right-hand side of the fireplace', and sometimes just the date, 'June 9th 1826'. I always felt that this was one up for the barely literate and poorly paid mount cutters whose quirky copperplate handwriting I borrowed for the purpose. I also found it useful to discover where a certain artist was living

or even on holiday on a particular date during the nineteenth century. Art scholars are so thorough these days that they are likely to know what Degas had for breakfast on 4 January 1874. So with the help of a book by some reputable author I might find out that Kees van Dongen was visiting Matisse in Paris during the summer of 1924 and then make some reference to it, in French, on the back of my Sexton.

I do not speak French or German, but with the help of foreign language phrase books I have always been able to come up with something to put on the back of French Impressionists like Degas, Renoir and Sisley - and German Expressionists like Feininger, Nolde and Munch.

Why is it that dealers always seem to set so much store by this kind of thing, when the paper I did it on was probably made in England in 1940 or 1950, is a mystery to me. I suppose the short answer is that it takes a brave man to destroy a fake, particularly if he is in the business of buying and selling pictures.

It is only human to make mistakes from time to time; I would myself if I was an art dealer. It is impossible for any man to know everything about pictures and I doubt if there is a dealer anywhere in the world who hasn't unknowingly, and sometimes knowingly, had Sextons passing through his hands. But few if any of them will admit the mistake and say: 'Okay, I've been fooled. I'll be more careful next time.' They feel that their reputations are at stake, so they wriggle around like eels and shout and scream denials until they are blue in the face.

I have already mentioned Jim the Penman and that signing pictures is a trade practice in the art world. Painters go in and out of fashion almost as regularly as women's clothes. Even great artists like Turner have had their ups and downs. This often gives rise to the even more crafty practice of taking a signature off rather than putting one on. If, for example, a *genre* painter like Vermeer is rediscovered and becomes greatly sought after, a dealer might ask a restorer to paint out the signature on a similar painting by De Hoogh and put in Vermeer's. Further, he might take the signature off a minor German Impressionist and leave it unsigned in the hope that it might pass for a French one.

To me the greatest achievement and thrill is if one of my Sexton Blakes can get by the experts *without* Michelangelo's signature at the bottom.

Goya ☐	Nolde ☐	De Hoogh ☐
Rembrandt ☐	Van Gogh ☐	El Greco ☐
Feininger ☐	Tintoretto ☐	Matisse ☐
Degas ☐	Palmer ☐	Munch ☐
Renoir ☐	Sisley ☐	
Michelangelo ☐	Vermeer ☐	

7 Read these statements carefully. Read the text again and decide which statements are true and which are false.

1 When Tom Keating claimed that the great masters painted through him, people were rather sceptical. They believed him, however, when they saw the paintings.

2 Tom Keating believes that there are traces of the great painters' spirits in the physical material of their paintings.

3 He produced a Degas pastel one night during a period of illness.

4 He claims that he has no control over his ability to paint like the old masters.

5 He claims that there is always something special about the paintings that came down to him from the great painters.

6 He sometimes deliberately painted badly so that the experts would know that his paintings weren't by the original artist.

7 He aimed to fool experts by writing messages on the back of some of his paintings.

8 He says that even though dealers knew that the paper he used was quite recent they were still fooled by the messages they found in foreign languages on the back of the paintings.

9 He says that art dealers don't admit to having bought fakes because they don't want to look stupid.

10 It is common practice in the art trade to pass off paintings as being from a different county of origin.

Unit 14

Phrasal verbs `pass`

In the Tom Keating extract the phrasal verb *pass for* is used meaning 'to appear to be'.
The verb *pass* can also be used with these particles to make other phrasal verbs:

> along round as away between by down
> for off on out over through to under up

8 Complete these sentences with the correct particles.

1 When we were children we only had clothes which other people passed _____ to us.
2 Alan was passed _____ when it came to promotion to manager and he left the company shortly after.
3 She never passes _____ the chance to eat out in a restaurant, so she has accepted our invitation.
4 The letters that passed _____ them became shorter and shorter over the years.
5 My favourite uncle passed _____ last year. He was 87 years old and had had a very full life, so we were not too upset.
6 When I ran into the back of the bus, my head hit the windscreen and I passed _____ .
7 This painting was passed _____ as an original Gauguin and sold for a fortune.
8 Pass _____ those crisps, please. I'm starving!

9 Now write context sentences for the particles you didn't use in Exercise 8.

Idioms `have`

> In the Tom Keating extract *have* is used idiomatically in the expression 'ever been had'. In this case *had* means 'fooled' or 'deceived'.

10 Look at these other idiomatic uses of *have*. Write a definition for each expression.

1 Indurain made a break from the bunch after 50 kilometres, **putting everything he had into it**.
2 He **was had up for** stealing a car and given six months in prison.
3 That's the third time this week that the television has broken down. I think **it's had it**.
4 Dawn **had it in for me** from the moment I arrived and did everything she could to make life difficult for me.
5 I never thought Michael **had it in him** to become a champion cross country runner.
6 I can't stand people who sulk - I'd much rather **have it out** straight away and get it over with.

Grammar `as and like`

11 Complete these sentences with a suitable word or phrase beginning with *as* or *like*.

1 When I was younger I worked...
2 Your face is red. You look...
3 He had to go to hospital...
4 I really like modern music,...
5 I was late for the concert and I got there...
6 Where's Andrew? Oh! That sounds...
7 The news of her promotion came...
8 When I left they gave me a cake as big...

"Was he as short as that in real life?"

Writing   dialogue

Look at this painting by the British artist, William Hogarth (1697-1764).

12 What do you think the people are saying to each other?

Here are some possible topics of conversation:

- people they know
- something going on outside
- a business arrangement
- something that is going to happen in the future
- family life

Write a dialogue between the people. Give them names and set your dialogue out as on page 110 of your Students' Book.

Extension and consolidation

Editing

1 There is an extra word in each line of this text. Put a line through the extra word and write it in the space on the right.

On an aeroplane you're helpless. The film you're see is somebody   1_____
else's choice, and it usually has the George Segal in it. Once I   2_____
watched a whole of movie with the wrong soundtrack. It was Fletch,   3_____
and when Chevy Chase spoke it was Julie Andrews who came from   4_____
out of his mouth.
You're trapped in the your headphones and trapped in your seat. You   5_____
feel helpless, too, because you're watching at it in danger.   6_____
Cinemas are safe, that it is one of their charms. They're dark and   7_____
upholstered and warm as the womb. Theres are staff with the uniforms   8_____
to look after of you. A plane cabin tries to fool you with the   9_____
same set-up, but suddenly it meets a turbulence, bumps and jolts,   10_____
and three hundred of you are sit there thinking of the drop beneath.   11_____
In the middle of *A Man For All The Seasons* there's a ping, and on   12_____
come the little red signs: FASTEN YOUR SEATBELTS. In the front   13_____
of the celluloid swordfight are three hundred souls fear for their   14_____
lives.

Dictation

2 Read the Tom Keating extract below. Each gap represents three words. Try to fill in the words. Use a pencil.

_____ tuberculosis in 1802 at the age of twenty-seven. 'If Tom Girtin had lived,' said Turner at his funeral, 'I _____ .'

   I very much doubt whether Turner would have lacked admirers even if _____ on. But Turner recognised his friend's genius and I agree that Girtin was _____ , at least at that time. Although _____ a few Sextons of Turner, I have always _____ by Girtin.

   In those early days all _____ do was emulate the masters. I felt that I could achieve this far more successfully by _____ materials as they did. I have never wanted to make money out of their work _____ buy grand pianos or even a mouth organ; I just _____ to paint like them.

3 [S35] Now listen to a recording of the extract. Complete the extract with the original words.

Tapescript of Student's Cassette

S1

When you happen to step off an edge you didn't see and lurch forward into space waving your arms, it's the end of the world for a second or two, and after you do land, even if you know you're okay and no bones are broken, it may take a few seconds to decide whether this is funny or not. Your body is still worked up about the fall – especially the nervous system and the adrenaline-producing areas. In fact, I am still a little shaky from a spill that occurred two hours ago, when I put on a jacket, walked out the front door of this house and for no reason whatever took a plunge down five steps and landed on the sidewalk flat on my back with my legs in the air. I am in fairly good shape, not prone to blackouts or sudden dizziness, and a sudden inexplicable fall comes as a big surprise to me.

A woman who was jogging down the street – a short, muscular young woman in a grey sweatshirt and sweatpants – stopped and asked if I was okay. 'Yeah! Fine!' I said and got right up. 'I just fell, I guess,' I said. 'Thanks,' I said. She smiled and trotted away.

Her smile has followed me into the house, and I see it now as a smirk, which is what it was. She was too polite to bend over and hoot and shriek and guffaw and cackle and cough and whoop and wheeze and slap her thighs and stomp on the ground, but it was all there in the smile: she perceived this as symbolic political theatre, whereas I saw it as something which was actually happening to me at the time. I suppose I could have understood that the sight of a tall man in a suit folding up and waving his arms and falling helplessly and landing flat on his back was the punchline of a joke she had been carrying around with her for a long time.

I might have seen it her way, but she ran down the street, and now I can only see my side of the fall, and feel cheapened by the whole experience. I understand now why my son was so angry with me a few months ago when he tripped on a shoelace and fell in the neighbour's yard – a yard where the neighbour's sheepdog had lived for years – and I laughed at him.

'It's not funny!' he yelled.

'Oh, don't be so sensitive,' I said.

Don't be so sensitive! What a dumb thing to say! Who has the right to tell someone else how to feel? It is the right of the person who falls on the dog droppings to decide for himself or herself how he or she will feel. It's not up to a jury. The fallen person determines whether it's funny or not.

S2

1 /iː/ ski, encyclopaedia, analyses, ceiling, key
2 /ɪ/ movies, orange, mountain, village, pretty, started, wicked, supposedly
3 /e/ many, leisure, leopard, friend
4 /æ/ passion, plaid
5 /ɑː/ demand, ask, aunt, clerk, reservoir, heart
6 /ɒ/ sausage, rendezvous, gone, cough, knowledge
7 /ɔː/ broad, door, restore, drawer
8 /ʊ/ full, push, cook, would, woman
9 /uː/ do, move, shoe, rheumatism, two
10 /ʌ/ come, mother, couple, flood, does

a floor (7) b litre (1) c image (2) d southern (10) e who (9)
f Gloucester (6) g pudding (8) h sergeant (5) i says (3)

S3

Brian Redhead It's eight o'clock on Thursday the twenty-sixth of November. Two hundred people have been killed by a typhoon in the Philippines and there are fears of many more casualties. The amateur athletics board has published the names of 133 British athletes who have passed random drug tests, six refused to take a test and retired.

Today's newsreader is Brian Perkins.

Perkins A powerful typhoon has struck the east coast of the Philippines and first reports indicate that many people have been killed. The worst affected area is the province of Sorsogon. So far it's been impossible for government and Red Cross officials to verify the number of casualties as power lines are down and roads and bridges into the region are destroyed. It's thought most of the victims lived in coastal shanty settlements which were swept away by huge waves whipped up by winds approaching 130 miles an hour. From Manilla, Humphrey Hawksley:

Hawksley Reports from the area affected by typhoon Nina are sketchy but the manager of the local Catholic radio station Mr Gerard De Bisa said he believed as many as 200 people were dead. Bodies were being brought to the provincial capital of Sorsogon for a burial mass in the evening. He could not confirm reports that up to 1,600 people were either dead or missing but Mr De Bisa said that a coastal area with a population of 70,000 people, mainly fishing families, had been badly flooded. He said that an estimated 90% of property there, mainly coastal shanty settlements had been destroyed and that hundreds of people were missing.

Perkins The six week old baby, David Barber, who had an operation at a Birmingham hospital yesterday to repair a hole in his heart, is said to be in a stable condition this morning. Doctors say the two and a half hour operation was very successful. The case gained national attention after the operation had been postponed five times because of a lack of trained nursing staff. The child's parents took the matter to the High Court where they failed to get an injunction forcing doctors to carry out the operation.

S4

Presenter The three thousand soldiers thought they were saved.
The sixth policeman threatened the safety of thousands.
Through thick and thin Cyril taught them theology.
Throughout the centuries these theories have thrived.

S5

Cardboard policemen have already been used to reduce shoplifting in supermarkets, and full-size cardboard patrol cars have been placed on motorway bridges. But police fear that SAM could be targeted by vandals if left alone on duty by the roadside. Mr Humphreys said: 'He's a futuristic model and could well become the second generation of the cardboard or plastic policemen. The concept is the same – people see a policeman and they react.'

S6

Dave Yes, most people who go to Spain go, and well, they perhaps fly out and then spend their time lying on the beach in the sun. Why did you choose to er, go on a cycling holiday, rather than having a beach holiday by the sea?

S/J It's something very different to any other type of holiday that I've had before and it's been a very long time since I have chosen to lie by the sea erm, on any kind of holiday. Most of my holidays have been walking and climbing in this country, in areas like the Yorkshire Dales and so on. I never really thought that I'd ever travel anywhere by bike and then, having met Nigel, who's a very keen cyclist, very experienced, I gradually got into the idea and managed to get the time off work and everything kind of fell into place. Erm, cycling sounded like a good thing to do. It was new and it was challenging. Having said that, on retrospect erm, I've seen other advantages to cycling now I've done it erm, I can see …

D What sort of things?

S/J In well, erm, from the moment I landed in Spain I felt very relaxed erm, mainly because it was just us and our bikes and we could go where we wanted to and we were very mobile. Erm, we didn't have the hassle of finding out trains or coaches or anything like that. We could just stop at a bar when we wanted to. Erm, we worked at our own pace – it was very relaxing. And also just being out there you're very much your – instead of just sitting inside a bus looking out, observing people, observing people walking up and down the roads or working in fields, you're actually out there being completely submerged in the environment. Erm, and both the social side of that and the physical environment side of it …

D So you think you met more Spanish people than if you'd been travelling by car, say.

S/J I, oh, most definitely. I can't see any value at all in driving up a mountain side in a car on a beautiful hot sunny day where you can't hear the birds and you can't hear the river rushing down the valley and I can't see any advantage to that.

D Perhaps the fact that you were cycling made people take more interest in you, do you think?

S/J Oh, I think so, I think you do get a certain amount of attention out there, particularly as I said earlier, because they are so keen on their cyclists. But yeah, people do take a lot more attention than just your normal average tourist – very interested in what you've been doing, where you've gone, how far you've gone, and how long you've taken to do it.

D So, it seems to have gone very smoothy, didn't you have any little disasters at all?

S/J Not any disasters, erm, as such. We had a few exciting moments. We were shot at on one occasion, just as we were getting into the tent.

D That sounds horrific!

S/J It was, it was fairly horrific and the shots were er, fairly close and erm, we don't know quite what was happening but we imagine it was in a hunting area and we imagine it was someone who'd heard rustling as we were putting up the tent and erm, thought there was something down there worth shooting and that er, we just kind of dived on the floor.

D So this was at night …

S/J Yeah, it was dark, and just very loud gunshots, very close – not knowing where …

D Did they hit the tent?

S/J No, they erm, we couldn't see anywhere where they'd hit. Erm, they hadn't done any damage to any of our things or to us, thank God.

D They didn't fire through your tyres and puncture them?

S/J No … no …

S7

1. They'll be **at** the office **at** the weekend too.
2. Alice comes **from** New York but I've no idea where Geoff comes from.
3. This was the first **of** five courses that he was going **to** attend.
4. I don't know what this is for. You'd better have a look **at** the instructions.
5. She's been working **for** the Ministry of Defence **for** six years now.
6. During their holiday in Spain they were shot at!

S8

Bhasi Kate, has anything amusing ever happened to you on your travels round the world?

Kate Quite a lot of things, I suppose. One thing that immediately springs to mind is when I was in Indonesia and er, I went with some friends to erm, visit a safari park and er, we were driving … it was quite a large park, and there were quite a few game-keepers around as well. Erm, and we drove into the lions' den, as it were. Erm, it was a closed-off area where lions were roaming free but there were also bears as well, close by erm, and we stopped to have a look at the bears because they were, they being quite friendly and quite a lot of cars were driving through the area. Erm, so we stopped the car, we were in a truck really, a sort of Land-Rover and erm, these bears came up to the car and er, I started to get a little bit worried about it. But they were OK. They didn't do anything. We thought they had just erm, looked at us and walked away, but we realised then that as we tried to drive off, we realised that one of the bears had actually eaten into erm, the two front tyres so we were stuck. Erm, we just couldn't drive off.

B Didn't you hear anything?

K No, we didn't hear anything at all, I mean they've obviously got such sharp teeth that er, they really just looked as though they were just bending down and not really doing anything – we didn't even feel it at all. It was only when we drove off that we realised that the two front tyres were completely flat. Er, so we had to try and signal to these game-keepers to er, to come and rescue us so they er, they arrived, three or four of them arrived with sticks to try and fend, to keep the animals back while we erm, got out of the car and they sort of escorted us out and then er, and then they changed the tyres for us and er, eventually we were able to drive off …

S9

1. There were quite a few game-keepers around as well.
2. It was a closed-off area where lions were roaming free but there were also bears as well.
3. We thought they had just erm, looked at us and walked away.
4. It was only when we drove off that we realised that the two front tyres were completely flat.
5. It was quicker if you let other people get off rather than trying to climb out …

S10

Only three yards away, behind the thick glass doors of the Sunday Times lobby, was the bright and comfortable world that suited most people well enough. I could see the commissionaire, smoothly uniformed behind his desk, looking forward to a pint of beer and an evening with the telly. People in sensible light-weight suits, with interesting jobs and homes to go to, flaunted their security at me and I felt my gut scream at me to strip off this ridiculous outfit and rush back into that light and the familiar interdependence. It struck me very forcefully that if I went on with this folly I would forever after be the man outside in the gutter looking in. For a moment I was lost beyond hope, utterly defeated.

Then I turned away from all that, somehow fumbled my packages away, got on the bike and set off in the general direction of the English Channel. Within minutes the great void inside me was filled by a rush of exultation, and in my solitary madness I started to sing.

S11

Conversation 1

Vicky So have you ever been conned?

Sheila Yes, I have. I blush to think about it. It was a pretty erm, dumb thing to have happened but erm, I was working for a publishing company then, and I was in reception at the time and I hadn't been working there for very long and somebody rang the intercom and said to me, 'I've got some curtains to deliver for the director of the company.' So I said, 'Fine.' And I let him in, and he came upstairs and said, 'It's a COD delivery and we need …' I don't remember the amount, sixty quid or something for the curtains … (COD? What's COD?) … Cash on Delivery. So I thought er, OK, erm, then I looked in the petty cash and there wasn't enough to cover it so erm, I said, 'Well I haven't got enough cash to pay Cash on Delivery,' so he said, 'Well, let me phone the director and erm, just confirm it with him and perhaps you can let me have a cheque or whatever.'

V So you were authorised to pay out to people who were delivering, etcetera.

S I thought I was. Erm, so I said, 'The director, Mr Francis, is at home at the moment, you can telephone him at home.' So this guy sat down opposite me, picked up the phone, made this phone call and had this conversation with Mr Francis erm, or so I thought. And erm, you know the conversation was well, fine, OK, so Sheila can give me a cheque for the sixty quid and that's OK, and fine. And he put the phone down and he said, 'Yeah, Mr Francis said that's fine.' So I got out the cheque book and I made out the cheque to this guy for sixty quid. There were some pre-signed cheques by one of, the business manager, I had to countersign, gave him the cheque and erm, he said, 'Right, well, I'll bring the curtains up in a sec.' And of course he went away and never pitched up again. And after a short while I phoned up Mr Francis and said, you know er, something strange has just happened and he said, 'I don't know what you're talking about. I haven't had any phone calls at all.' And this guy had been so smooth and I had been so green that he had pretended to make this telephone call to my boss in my presence and made this agreement that I was to give him a cheque. (And you didn't, you never suspected a thing.) Completely conned, completely conned.

V Oh, oh, that's terrible.

S Embarrassing really, to be so utterly stupid.

Conversation 2

Caroline So, Steve, have you ever been ripped off?

Steve Yes, erm, quite badly once. I was abroad and I was visiting some mountains erm, and I only had one day to visit them and I got to the place where the cable car goes up to the top of the mountain and the queue was huge, you know it was really long.

And they had these ticket touts … Now I'm always very wary of ticket touts, but 'cos the queue was so long and I only had that one day, I thought, well, it's worth it, you know, a bit of extra money, OK, but it means I can jump the queue. So I spoke to this man and we had trouble communicating but basically he said, you know, 'I've got a return ticket on this cable car. You can go up and see the views, come down and you won't have to queue at all.' Five minutes waiting maximum instead of four hours.
C What, people were actually queuing up to buy tickets?
S Yeah, there was about a four hour queue.
C But you could actually just walk on otherwise if you had a ticket.
S Yes, he'd obviously queued up earlier in the day and bought them, you see. (Presumably, yeah.) But obviously he said, you know, 'I am charging you more. I'm charging you about three times the price.' Well, you know, so it's once in a lifetime thing, let's do it, buy the ticket. And I got on the cable car within five minutes. That was fine. We got up to the top, wonderful views. It was only when I started to decide to come down and I went to the cable car and they said, 'Sorry, you've only got a one-way ticket.' And of course I couldn't contact the man 'cos he was down at the bottom of the mountain. He'd obviously gone home by then; he was having a cup of tea. So I had to buy another ticket to get back down off the mountain.
C So it cost you an awful lot more than you'd originally …
S Much more than I bargained for … a real mug.

S12

1 He was (a) bus driver.
2 There was (an) orange car outside.
3 (The) late edition, the early edition.
4 They bought (some) magazines.
5 Some people don't like the British.
6 Have you seen (his) new car?
7 She's a friend of his.
8 Explain to (her) her rights.
9 (Saint) Mark is one of the more popular saints.

S13

Victoria Well, Sandeep, I know your family's Hindu, but er, I'd really like to know a little bit about, you know, what it's like growing up in that sort of culture, you know, what it's like in terms of when you leave home and things like that. Can you tell me a bit about it?
Sandeep Yeah, sure. Well, it's different to English families, being Indian because well, erm, the boy, if the mother and the father have a son, the boy will leave home, well, he will never leave home. (Never leaves home?) He never will leave home because he will look after his mum and dad when they die. As for the girl, she will leave home when she gets married and goes off to her in-laws.
V Oh, right, so … but what about when the boy gets married?
S The boy, when the boy gets married, his wife comes home and lives with um, the in-laws, so it's … .
V Oh, I see … Right, so the, you don't get the chance to move out and go and move in with a few friends and get a flat and things? (No, no, we don't.) That would be unheard of in your culture.
S It isn't unheard of, but it's not Hindu religion, it's not our religion to do that. We have to look after our parents because when … it's like when we were kids they looked after us and now we do the same when they grow old, and we look after them.
V Mmm … but what about if, you know, your parents are really quite young, you know in their forties and you're already in your twenties and they don't really need looking after and you're not ready to get married, wouldn't it be possible to move out?
S Yes, then yeah, 'cos some people do move out, they have to move out er, you can move out but I wouldn't, not in my family. I would look after my mum and dad. Some families of my friends have already moved out, but not me. I'll look after my mum and dad.
V So would you say then that your family is fairly sort of er, strict – it sticks to the sort of hard-line Hindu …
S No … It's not strict. My family, no, we're not. My dad and mum are not strict.
V No, it's just your choice to stay there.
S Yeah, it's my choice.
V And what about your sisters? Do they, do they stay until they marry? (Yeah.) Or do they get the chance to move out and get a flat?
S Well, my sister wouldn't, no … (She wouldn't want to.) No, she'll move out when she gets married. Yes.
V What about other kinds of things when you were growing up? Did you erm, could you sort of start going out and becoming independent when you were quite young in your teens or were you sort of chaperoned by people or …?
S Well, my mum and dad gave me freedom when I were young, so you know, I could go out by myself to the shops and things like that, like some mums and dads used to go with them, so, but I never had the chance when I was younger about thirteen, fourteen, going out with my friends. My mum and dad don't let me …
V They wouldn't let you do that … When did they start letting you?
S Just about sixteen, seventeen now, just starting to let me out …
V Yeah, and was it different for your sister?
S Yeah, my sister is not allowed out. The Indian girls, they're not really allowed to go out. My mum and dad give her the freedom as well, as she works during the week so we're allowed out.

S14

1 He /hɪ/ said he /iː/ would see me later.
2 I often visit them (ðm) at weekends.
3 Did you see her (ɜː) at the party last night?
4 Let's (s) go and see Bert this afternoon.
5 There (ðe) were three cars parked outside.
6 Let us (ʌs) do the shopping today.
7 Look! She's over there. (ðeə)

S15

An American man who had lived for years in Japan explained a similar politeness ethic. He lived, as many Japanese do, in frightfully close quarters – a tiny room separated from neighbouring rooms by paper-thin walls. In this case the walls were literally made of paper. In order to preserve privacy in this most unprivate situation, his Japanese neighbours simply acted as if no one else lived there. They never showed signs of having overheard conversations, and if, while walking down the hall, they caught a neighbour with the door open, they steadfastly glued their gaze ahead as if they were alone in a desert.

S16

Caroline Right, Steve. What do you think style is?
Steve I think style is looking good in yourself. Erm, a lot of people confuse it with fashion and you know, what is fashionable to wear at the moment, but style, I think if you found something that you look good in, it suits you and you dress well, that's style. Or even just the way you live, the way you have, use your life, your lifestyle in general.
C OK. Erm, could you sort of give me an example? I mean what do you think is stylish and isn't stylish for you, for example?
S Er, for me, well I'm, I wouldn't, I'm not very into smart cars and, you know, and having all mod cons. Erm, I …
C So do you think that's not stylish?
S It's a different type of style, rather than not stylish. Erm, I know people who have lots of machinery in their bedrooms, you know, automatic CDs and remote controls everywhere. That's not my style. I'm much more basic. I like to have everything around me which I can actually see and use. It's not all machinery and technology …
C Right, so style for you would be different to style for someone else.
S Mmm … I mean a lot of people think, you know to have a good lifestyle it's got to be all fast cars, expensive clothes and rich food erm, and that sort of thing. Er, to me style is just erm, doing whatever you think's best for you and as I say for me it's basic things, basic needs. Yes, I need to eat but I don't need to spend fifty pounds on a bottle of champagne, that sort of thing.
C Right, so do you think that you lack in style, maybe? (Maybe I'm not very …) I hope that's not a personal comment but …
S Maybe I'm not very style conscious. I don't try too hard but then as I say, I think style is an individual thing. Er, and I don't like it when people try and impose their style on me and say well you don't wear the right sort of clothes or do the right sort of things …

S17

See page 39.

S18

Caroline So where do you come from?
Denis I'm originally from Doncaster, Yorkshire.
C And what are you doing in London?
D I came to London, in 1980 no, I'm sorry 1978, and er, when I came to London I came with a girl and we ended up going back to Yorkshire. And I came back to London again, and I stayed in a place called Centre Point. And I stayed there that much they actually turfed me out onto the streets and I stayed there too long. I tried to get accommodation in hotels and nobody'd take me in because I'd no deposit and everything. I had no ID, no way I could get ID, 'cos I couldn't afford it. So I ended up going all the way back to Yorkshire and er, getting a birth certificate and coming all the way, hitchhiking, back to London again.
C Did you have a job at that time?
D Not in the slightest, no.
C Did you … were you looking for jobs or did you not find anything?
D I was looking for work, but basically casual work, but with being at a young age, nobody really wanted to take me on.
C How old were you when you came down?
D I was about 18 or something like that.
C And so did you live on the streets at all then when you were kicked out?
D I spent just over a year and a half on the streets.
C And how old were you when you lived on the streets?
D 18-ish.
C How … what was it like?
D Er, summertime it was fine 'cos it was warm, but in the wintertime it was freezing. I was sleeping on the carriages (on the trains) on the trains, yeah, in Victoria Station on Platform 1. And sometimes you'd probably wake up at Dover in the morning, not realise you were there.
C Really? And what happened if you did that?
D Well we'd just run from the station so the police didn't get us and then hitchhike back to London.
C Yeah, erm, and what happened after that? How did you live?
D Erm, day centres, (For food and things like that?) begging, whatever you could do, you know, I mean I was never there stealing, so I never stole or anything like that – just begging, stuff like that, wandering around whatever.
C Yeah, and did you have a lot of friends at that time? Did you have sort of a group to support you?
D I wouldn't say many friends at all. I wouldn't class a lot of people on the streets as my friends because I couldn't trust them. (Really.) Yeah.
C Why? Because they could steal from you?
D 'Cos I didn't really know … 'cos there was a lot of thieves, a lot of drug addicts, alcoholics, you know and it was like, I didn't want to get involved with them that much. You know, just liked to talk to the girls on the station. They'd take you for teas and stuff like … take you for dinners. (That's nice.) More sympathy.
C Yeah, yeah, I can imagine. So erm, what happened after that? Did you ever have a job, did you ever work?
D Yeah, I actually found a job from a day centre called The Passage, and er, it was Sister Barbara and she was talking to somebody in the Job Centre about it and I actually went into a hotel, and I worked in a hotel as a night porter and I enjoyed that …

S19

(The letters which have a line through them are elided.)

nex~~t~~ turn	serve~~d~~ tea
gues~~t~~ house	len~~t~~ them
las~~t~~ week	sof~~t~~ drink
sen~~d~~ two	firs~~t~~ day
give him the book	Roger himself
cause~~d~~ conflict	nex~~t~~ day
spoil~~t~~ child	I've seen ~~h~~er twice
sen~~d~~ home	

S20

1 More fortunate than Ruffian is Rosemary, an angora rabbit from Stoke Newington in London currently enjoying a luxurious lifestyle.

2 To call Rosemary's garden dwelling a 'hutch' would be to undersell the property.

3 Its complex construction by a sculptor took three days.

4 Built from timber, it is over eight feet in length, with a corrugated plastic roof.

5 The front door is decorated with an eye, a heart and a rabbit, to signify 'I love bunnies', according to owner, Miss Robins.

6 The interior boasts walls decorated with plastic lettuce leaves and pictures of different types of rabbits.

7 If the temperature falls too low in winter, Miss Robins places a hot water bottle in a cake tin to keep the house warm.

S21

Caroline What's the worst place you've ever lived in?
Tony Erm … Well, it must be the first time I came to London. Erm, it was a house-share, there were three other guys erm, you know, four separate rooms. And erm, I mean I er, kind of pride myself on, I suppose, you know, neatness and cleanliness and tidiness and that kind of thing and they used to roll in at you know two, three in the morning with, and leave chips in the sink (oh no) and the bin used to be overflowing and you know, I'd go down in the morning, even if they made a cup of coffee they'd, you know, have a coffee in one place on the table with sugar on the other, all spilled on the table.
C Mmm … were you were you students? Because that's sort of notorious for students to be like that.
T Well, they were. Yeah, well, two or them were.
C Oh right, and you weren't.
T Well, we were all, I was just out of college, so we were all kind of, you know, 21, 22 type of age.
C Do you think it made a difference that you weren't a student?
T I don't know , I mean, I, I've always been kind of clean, I suppose.
C Right … even when you were a student.
T Yeah. Erm, and then I think the worst episode I remember was you know, the landlord said, no, I said to the landlord, you know, I need a little coffee table and he said, 'OK, get it from Simon's room, it's at the end of his room, you know, just kind of you know, walk in, here's the key and get the coffee table.' So the landlord stood outside the room and I was in my bare feet. I'd just come out of the shower. And I was, you know, tiptoeing across his room and the smell was terrible, anyway it was … (Why?) things were, I don't know, the windows were closed; it smelt kind of dank, it was, you know, a really humid kind of claustrophobic atmosphere. Erm, and there were horrible things around. I remember seeing a bowl of you know, cornflakes, a breakfast cereal, that had turned blue. (Oh, what with mould?) And mould on the top. (Oh how disgusting!) And there was a kind of … the bedspread and the sheets were all around the room, you kind of, you know, stood on strange things. And I was walking across the room in my bare feet and I stood on something and I, it squelched, you know, it kind of it stuck to my foot. (What was it?) Erm, well I looked down in in kind of horror really, 'cos I kind of turned my foot up and it, it was a kind of off-blue-green pork chop, you know, hanging from my foot. And I just kind of, and I just kind of ran out of the room really but I just remember this smell and the whole room being horrible.
C That's disgusting!
T Oh yeah, you know, records out of sleeves and that kind of thing.
C And this pork chop had been, had it been there for quite some time?
T Oh, probably weeks, weeks. And you know he had various girlfriends and stuff like that which I could never erm …
C Understand …
T Never understand … yeah, it was weird …

S22

1 I woke my sister <u>up</u>, then went and had breakfast.

2. They always got up late on Sundays, never before midday.
3. Turn off the TV, will you? It's getting on my nerves.
4. You can come in now, Henry.
5. Come in. I'm sorry to have kept you waiting.
6. He switched on the engines and the plane took off.

S23

Johnathan I don't tend to … I don't think I tend to get depressed for very long. I sort of, I get down then I get up, but I don't really sort of get depressed for very long. I know people who do, I mean, like my girlfriend gets depressed sometimes. I find that quite hard actually.
Joanne How do you deal with it? I mean, what do you do to help her?
John You just have to give them time and space and you just have to realise that you know they're going to be negative for a couple of days about or however long and then, you know, sort of gradually they'll get over it. I don't know, I wouldn't know how to deal with it if it was a sort of clinical depression or they really got seriously depressed.
Joanne How long would you put up with it, do you think is a reasonable time to actually try and understand. Would you give it a time limit …?
John I don't think you put a time limit on these things, you just you know, play it by ear and could be a week, could be two weeks. I don't know, I've never actually sort of lived with, I remember living with one guy at university … he was depressed all the time. But that just became a joke eventually. (Right – he was depressed all the time.) Yeah, right, exactly. You know, like absolutely nothing would make him happy.
Joanne Right, but they do say about depressed people, they get really high as well. Did he get, was he very happy some of the time, as well?
John Once, maybe.
Joanne What, in three years?
John Yeah, I don't think I ever saw him happy.
Joanne Oh, that sounds awful.

S24

1. I don't think I tend to get depressed for very long.
2. I mean, what do you do to help her?
3. … you just play it by ear and could be a week, could be two weeks, you just have to realise that you know they're going to be negative for a couple of days about or however long and then, you know, sort of gradually they'll get over it.

S25

It's taken me twenty years to discover that the best way to avoid this is to throw the whole bulky package away. Don't do that stuff any more. Go somewhere where you can't get hold of it, where they don't have a radio or a TV or a telephone or even a bathroom mirror to contemplate. Some people call this running away, but I've come to regard it as a basic and healthy reflex. You find what's hurting you – fantasy overload – and you move away from the source of the pain.

S26

Author The rustle of the palm trees in the light breeze provided a pleasing accompaniment to the unceasing rhythm of the waves. Sunlight played on the water, highlighting the azure depths. Amanda stretched comfortably on the lounger, trying to decide whether she had time for another dip before getting ready to go to the barbecue.

The factory seemed at its greyest in the pouring rain, Amanda reflected, as she got out of the car and locked it. It didn't look much better inside. The machinery was out of date and the walls were peeling. It was all rather Dickensian. But no doubt the new owner would soon set the place to rights.

Narrator We're often asked what sort of background is most popular with readers of Mills and Boon. A sophisticated setting, perhaps an international resort like Acapulco where the jetset live, or the great outdoors, like a logging camp in the tropical rainforest. Or maybe a houseboat on a magical lake in Kashmir. All these backgrounds have been used successfully by our authors. But books set in what might be considered much less glamorous places: a light-engineering factory in the Midlands, a lawyer's office in London, a woollen mill in Yorkshire, have been equally successful.

Remember that Mills and Boon readers live all over the world and what may seem a glamorous setting to one is quite ordinary to another. An Indian reader once surprised us by demanding less stories about the exotic East and more books about Scotland, please. And a reader from New Zealand who was actually married to a sheep-farmer begged us: 'No more books about sheep stations. They're the most unromantic place you can imagine.'

The one important thing to remember is that which ever background you choose, it should be as accurate as you can possibly make it. Write about what you know, is a sound rule to follow. Especially when you're just beginning as an author. If you've never worked in an office and haven't the faintest idea about the day-to-day duties involved, don't set a book there and make your heroine a secretary. Any reader who's familiar with the scene will wince at every mistake and her pleasure in the story will be ruined. You'd be surprised how many would-be authors ignore this glaringly obvious advice.

Author 'I wonder if you would be interested in reading my book, 'Tigers on his track'. The story is set on an Australian cattle station and concerns the efforts of the hero to save his livestock from the wild tigers which live in the bush.'

Narrator It was never published. Like the book that was set in Venice and had the hero taking the heroine on a sightseeing tour in his red sports car. A dampening experience! So remember, if your hero walks down the main street in Bognor Regis and checks his watch with the townhall clock clearly visible on the skyline, make sure you've got your facts right!

S27

Narrator
1. Amanda stretched comfortably on the lounger, trying to decide whether she had (w) time for another dip before getting ready to go to the barbecue.
2. The machinery was (w) out of the date and the walls were (w) peeling.
3. But no doubt the new owner would (s) soon set the place to rights.
4. We're (w) often asked what sort of background is (s) most popular with readers of Mills and Boon.
5. A light-engineering factory in the Midlands, a lawyer's office in London, a woollen mill in Yorkshire, have (s) been equally successful.
6. Remember that Mills and Boon readers live all over the world and what may (s) seem a glamorous setting to one is quite ordinary to another.
7. Whichever background you choose, it should be as accurate as you can (w) possibly make it …
8. 'I wonder if you would (s) be interested in reading my book.'

S28

Maria I can say I enjoyed my primary education quite a lot because I went to school in the village where I lived and er, it was very varied experience because er, we were boys and girls, boys and girls from any social class so all of them brought different experiences into the classroom. That was interesting; also the teacher was a good one. We felt very secure with her and erm, and everything went well I think, while when I passed to secondary education, I changed town, I went to another town and er, the school was completely different. We were only girls and we had very strict teachers. I think life didn't come into the school at that time. School was something and life was something else – completely opposite to the primary course and erm, I don't remember that part of my education as a good part, as a lively part, a part which enriched my personality. After that I went to – how can I call it, Liceo, second part of secondary school, second level and er, it was still different from the other two. We were boys and girls again but I lived that experience in a very difficult period because it was around 1968. I mean, difficult for some reasons and er, enjoyable for some others. Mostly enjoyable because something new was entering the school. New ideas, new aspects of personality were taken into consideration in those times but difficult because everything tended to be sided by politics, every single thing was – had to do with politics and so either you committed yourself in politics a lot or you, you felt out of some of the experiences we had there. This is what concerns my relationship with the rest of the class. Erm, as concerns the teachers, I don't remember so many of them with pleasure and enjoyment. Most of them tended to give just lessons and nothing else. They didn't give themselves into the experience of daily, daily education and that's all before university. The experience of university instead was a good one I think, because it was a very small course I'd say. We were only about twenty people which is … which is good, I mean because most of the people when they go university tend to have classes of two hundred or three hundred, sometimes they do not even see the teacher. The teacher is in another classroom, and they just, they can just hear the teacher while speaking. It was a little bit like Liceo sometimes while we also had some very good relationships with some of the teachers and if I have to conclude by saying what education has left … has left me I would say that at least it has given me an idea of what to do in class now while teaching and what not to do at the same time, but I think that education can … is still going on. I mean – can go on in the school or in any other place and maybe is now going on with more tolerance I would say, with more freedom and with more interest.

S29

1 What was certain, was that this had been the worst recession since the War.
2 I can't see the **difference** between studying English at school and studying it in **England**.
3 **Patience** is one of the most useful qualities in a language teacher.
4 Alternative **medicine** has become very popular in **Britain** over the last few years.
5 It might be **prudent** to book tickets for the train as it's a Bank Holiday.
6 We have had correspondence with the owners of the supermarket and we are now waiting for a decision.

S30

This Friday, the Irish president will present American author Norman Rush with the *Irish Times*-Aer Lingus International Fiction Prize (a cool twenty-five thousand pounds) for his novel, *Mating*. I was one of the five judges, which involved flying First Class to Dublin several times, eating at expensive restaurants and – the down side – reading forty-six books. Normally it would take me at least four years to read forty-six books. Not only that, but at the discussion meetings we were called upon to give little speeches, off the cuff, on our favourites or rejects. I am no orator; everything I say needs rewrites. The fee was a lure, but a friend calculated that at the rate I was reading I was being paid about twenty pence an hour.

S31

1 Look at the page – she'd better come – She's in Paris
2 The first year – I've found you at last
3 Students showed their work – In case you get there late
   Here's your lunch – He was shown to his room.
4 Not quite – He would get there late – She was thrown clear
   They won't get a rise.

S32

Paul When I was a child in er, Richmond there were er, three cinemas and er, they were called The Ritz, er, The Gaumont and The Odeon. The Ritz was probably the most modern but that was bulldozed back in the er, the 60s – it was made into er, office blocks. The Gaumont was the scruffiest cinema and we used to call it the 'flea-pit' erm, and the façade is still there – it's offices now but that was er, demolished in the 70s and the Odeon, which was probably the most beautiful cinema, and erm, that's still there, although it's been divided into a three-screen cinema. The architecture's still intact and er, it's got this beautiful interior.

The first film I ever went to was erm, well the first one I can remember anyway, was a Western starring John Wayne and it was called *The Commancheros* and I went and saw that in Hammersmith with my parents. And another one that I remember vaguely was about submarines and about the war in the Pacific and I remember it had James Garner in it – he must have been very young at the time. I developed a passion for the cinema and erm, when I was quite young, when I was a student I worked at Sainsbury's which is a supermarket and erm, Sainsbury's used to be closed on Mondays so I had er, I had Mondays free and none of my friends were free so I used to spend my time going to the cinema and I used to see one film in the afternoon and then move on to see another film in the evening. I probably spent most of my money going to the cinema.

And then later when I went to University – I went to University in Aberystwyth. Now in Aberystwyth in the evenings there's nothing much to do really apart from go to the pub or go to the cinema. There, there were three cinemas, the Conway, the Cambrian and the Celtic. I believe some of them are still there. And er, here was my first contact with audience participation. Er, students used to let off energy during the short films which showed before the main feature and they were always very obscure things like *Pipe-laying in Siberia* and er, it was a sort of a competition to shout the funniest comment er, as the film was being shown. And I remember one evening – I had never seen *Ben Hur* so I went to the Cambrian to see *Ben Hur* and it was a very decrepit cinema where there were seats missing. You never knew when you went into the cinema in the dark and sat down whether you'd actually find a seat there and erm, anyway we were watching *Ben Hur* and during the chariot race when the sound system was just barely able to cope with the noise er, a section of the ceiling came down and covered everybody in the first three rows with plaster.

S33

1 In <u>November</u> there <u>was</u> the <u>annual</u> visit by the <u>owner</u> <u>of</u> <u>the</u> factory.
2 <u>Actually</u> she's not <u>as</u> <u>introverted</u> as she might seem <u>at</u> first.
3 We had a very <u>romantic</u> evening <u>at</u> <u>a</u> new restaurant in <u>the</u> <u>centre</u> of <u>London</u>.
4 She's <u>a</u> <u>brilliant</u> pianist who studied <u>at</u> <u>the</u> <u>Conservatory</u> in Paris.
5 <u>Property</u> is <u>the</u> most valuable asset during times <u>of</u> <u>monetary</u> <u>instability</u>.

S34

Paul Can you tell me something about your job at the Hayward Gallery?
Henry Well, I'm talking over at the Hayward Gallery next month, as you know. Erm, and it's really, there are really three parts to the job, one of which is running the Hayward Gallery itself, and the second of which is the er … National Touring Exhibitions programme and the third (Can you … sorry, yes, you'll explain that in a minute …) is the er, Arts Council collection. The Hayward is a er, very large machine, if you like – it er, runs about four large exhibitions a year or rather more if one considers that sometimes the space is divided into two parts, one exhibition on the ground floor like the Mexican show at the moment and the second exhibition upstairs at the moment that's an exh … a showing of Bridget Riley's recent abstract paintings.
P And what in your opinion are the strong and the weak points in the Gallery and the collection?
H The Gallery, the Gallery's not terribly flexible er, internally, the problem is restricted access so one can't close down different parts of the building and er, at one time. So in practice it means you've got to have an exhibition occupying both floors fully or at least occupying each of the two floors separately and, and this inter … there's very limited storage space. So it means you have to spend two or three weeks between exhibitions for the turnround so that, that's it, can be a …
P So the Gallery has to stay closed while you're preparing the new exhibition …
H Yes … so you have to stay closed and that of course is … er, deters erm, the public and they don't come on spec in the hope that they'll see something there, they have to trek …
P Yes, that's true I suppose it could be off-putting.
H And the other thing of course is that it is erm, the walkways and the approaches are fairly unhospitable and windswept but I think they will something will probably have to be done about those.

P Yes, yes ...
H There are plans, there is talk of rebuilding the Hayward Gallery and I'm sure that there'll be serious discussion over the next five years but there's not, there's no guarantee of government funding and of course the problem at the moment with mixed developments is that the economy is doing so badly that it's very difficult to find suitable partners.
P Yes, I can imagine. Yes.
H But the situation, the site is a very good one and when you think that the er, the newest in fact the first er, mainline railway terminal to be built in Britain in this century I think, is just being completed at Waterloo and that'll of course bring people over from the er ...
P ... the Continent ...

[S35]
Girtin died of tuberculosis in 1802 at the age of twenty-seven. 'If Tom Girtin had lived,' said Turner at his funeral. 'I should have starved.'

I very much doubt whether Turner would have lacked admirers even if Girtin had lived on. But Turner recognised his friend's genius and I agree that Girtin was the greater artist, at least at that time. Although I have done a few Sextons of Turner, I have always been more interested by Girtin.

In those early days all I wanted to do was emulate the masters. I felt that I could achieve this far more successfully by using the same materials as they did. I have never wanted to make money out of their work with which to buy grand pianos or even a mouth organ; I just wanted to learn to paint like them.

Answer Key

Unit 1

Vocabulary development

1 Look back at page 6 of your Students' Book to check your answers.

Vocabulary building

2 1 The *-e* becomes *-y*.
2 Add *-y*. If the vowel preceding the final *-b*, *-d*, *-g*, *-n* or *-t* is a short one, double this consonant as well.

cloudy foggy rainy sunny thirsty muddy

There are no fixed answers for the final part of this exercise. Check your answers in a dictionary.

Listening

4 1 3 5 8
5 Check your answers by looking at the tapescript [S1].

Idioms

6 1 b 2 c 3 a 4 c 5 b

Pronunciation

8 Check your answers by looking at the tapescript [S2].

Reading

10 2 exotic 3 reflect 4 Several 5 sense 6 encouraged
7 while 8 favourite 9 keen 10 wants 11 sufficiently
12 work 13 Mind 14 seriously 15 even

Phrasal verbs

11 to obtain or acquire casually: **to pick up**
to produce or find: **to come up with**
1 came 2 coming 3 pick 4 come 5 picking 6 come
7 picked 8 comes 9 picked 10 picked

Grammar

12 1 E, F 2 F 3 C 4 H 5 I
Hand your sentences to your teacher for checking.

13 1 The earth **rotates** in a **clockwise** direction.
2 When **hot** air **rises** it gets **colder**.
3 The sea **rises** and **falls** according to the phases of the **moon**.
4 A **solar** eclipse occurs when the moon **passes** between the sun and the earth.
5 Water **boils** at a temperature of **100** degrees centigrade.

14 This man's **driving** along a country road one day when he **looks** in his rear-view mirror and **sees** a police car following him. He **checks** his speed and **slows** down but the police car still **follows** him. After another mile the police car **overtakes** him and **stops** him. The policeman **gets** out and **comes** up to the car. The man **winds** down the window and **says**, 'Can I help you, Officer?' and the policeman **answers**, 'We picked up a woman a mile or two back who claims to be your wife. She says that she fell out of your car.' And the man **replies**, 'Oh, thank goodness for that! I thought I'd gone deaf!'

Writing

15 Here is the correct version of the letter. Don't worry if there is some variation in your version. If you have any doubts, check with your teacher.

```
                                        TSB Bank
                                        PO Box 397
                                        London
                                        NW6 3JJ
                                        Tel: 071 723 7171
                                        Fax: 071 723 2972

Ref AGJ/TK/IF/r
22 December 1992

Mr P Miller
88 Aberdeen Road
Kensington
London
W8 31Y

Dear Mr Miller

I am pleased to acknowledge receipt of your application for
a new cheque book.

However, upon checking our records I note that a cheque book
was forwarded to you in June 1992. None of these cheques have
been presented and I would, therefore, appreciate it if you
would advise me if you have or have not received this book.
If not, please contact me immediately and I will arrange for
a stop to be placed upon it and a new book ordered for you.

I have enclosed a Eurocheque Card Application and would be
grateful if you would complete and return the form to us.

I look forward to hearing from you.

Yours sincerely


New Accounts Dept
Overseas Branch

enc
```

Unit 2

Vocabulary development
Hand your sentences to your teacher for checking.

Vocabulary building
2
List A	List B
security	morality
brutality	personality
familiarity	majority
sensitivity	minority
superiority	publicity
generosity	principality
simplicity	priority
formality	

Listening
3
- 8 time of the news broadcast
- 26 date of the news broadcast
- 2.5 length in hours of an operation
- 200 number of people killed by a typhoon
- 90 percentage of properties destroyed by a typhoon
- 1600 number of people missing or dead
- 130 speed of winds in miles per hour
- 133 number of British athletes tested for drug abuse
- 6 age of the person operated on
- 5 number of times they postponed the operation

4 See tapescript S3.

Pronunciation
5 Check your answers by looking at the tapescript S4.

Grammar
6 There is, for example, the case of the theologian which I **described** in 'Archetypes of the Collective Unconscious'. He **had** a certain dream that he **was standing** on a slope from which he **had** a beautiful view of a low valley covered with dense woods. In the dream he **knew** that in the middle of the woods there **was** a lake, and he also **knew** that hitherto something **had** always **prevented** him from going there. But this time he **wanted** to carry out his plan. As he **approached** the lake, the atmosphere **grew** uncanny, and suddenly a light gust of wind **passed** over the surface of the water, which **rippled** darkly. He **awoke** with a cry of terror.

7 Hand your sentences to your teacher for checking.

Reading
8 B E A D C

9
1. The links between cancer and radiation.
2. Because doctors in the fourteenth century were just as baffled by the Black Death as doctors in the twentieth century are by cancer.
3. That they are not in fact safe and that they are only said to be safe for economic reasons.

10
1. Radioactive fallout from the Windscale disaster of 1957.
2. By pretending it was less serious than it was and giving the public wrong information about it.
3. It has tried to convince the public that nuclear power is quite safe.

11 atomic radiation, nuclear power, nuclear reactors, radioactive cloud, meltdown, nuclear fuels

12 1 radiation 2 reactors 3 radioactive 4 meltdown

Idioms
13 (Sample sentences.)
1. I'm unhappy, bored and tired as a result of people complaining.
2. I know it's a lot of work but I like a job I can do with maximum involvement and energy.
3. The proposed new motorway would go right past her house. She will do everything she can to stop it.

Phrasal verbs
14 1 turn back 2 turn down 3 turn in 4 turn off 5 turn up

Hand your sentences to your teacher for checking.

Grammar
15 Hand your noun phrases to your teacher for checking.

Writing
16 Hand your letter to your teacher for checking.

17 Hand your small ad to your teacher for checking.

Extension and consolidation

Editing
1
Britain's first robot policeman was unveiled yesterday * the West Mercia force. SAM (Speed and Aggression Moderator), * was holding a radar gun, could eventually appear * kerbsides to deter speeding motorists. SAM is five foot seven and * half inches tall, wears uniform and has a papier-mâché head * turns slowly, powered * a small battery-charged engine.
Chief Supt Brian Humphreys, West Mercia's head * traffic, said: 'SAM moves faster than * real thing.'
The robot went on show * the launch of the force's new offensive against aggressive drivers. Public reaction * the idea of sending SAM on the beat will be gauged * displaying him at exhibitions this summer.

1 by 2 who 3 at 4 a 5 that 6 by 7 of 8 the 9 at 10 to 11 by

Dictation
2 Check your answers by looking at the tapescript S5.

Unit 3

Vocabulary development
1 Look back at page 22 of your Students' Book to check your answers.

2 Hand your sentences to your teacher for checking.

Vocabulary building
3 renaissance (x) grievance (x) brilliant (a) maintain (v) intolerant (a) reluctant (a) enter (v) disturb (v) accordance (x) apply (v) disappear (v)

4
1. maintenance
2. entrance
3. intolerance
4. reluctance
5. brilliance
6. appliances

Listening
5 1, 2, 3, 4, 7 and 8 are false.
5 and 6 are true.

6 1 False. She says it has been a very long time since she has been on a beach holiday, not that she has never been on one.
2 False. What she says implies that her friend, Nigel, an experienced cyclist, encouraged her to go.
3 False. She says that it was a good thing they were on bicycles because they didn't have to find out train times and this implies they didn't use the train.
4 False. She doesn't say this in the text.
5 True. She says she can see no advantage in going up a mountain in a car on a sunny day.
6 True. She says 'they are so keen on their cyclists' and also that people were interested in them and their journey.
7 False. She says that they imagined they were in a hunting area but only after they were shot at.
8 False. She says that there was no damage to themselves or their things.

7 Advantages of a cycling holiday:
new and challenging
made her feel relaxed
very mobile
no hassle with timetables
could stop when they liked
went at their own pace
submerged in the environment rather than spectators
more contact with local people

Idioms

8 1C 2H 3E 4A 5G 6B 7D 8I 9F

9 Check your answers by looking at the tapescript S7 .

Reading

10 1G 2D 3I 5E 6J 7C 8F 9A 10H

11 2

Hand your sentence to your teacher for checking.

Phrasal verbs

12 Hand your sentences to your teacher for checking.

13 (Sample sentences.)

1 I got on the plane at Milan and arrived in London an hour and a half later.
2 As soon as she heard about the accident Sheila got on the phone to her mother.
3 He got his mac and wellingtons on and went out into the rainy night.
4 He told me to get on with my work or he'd report me to the manager.
5 How are you getting on with the plans for the new supermarket?
6 Even though he only qualified last year he is getting on very well and may get promotion soon.
7 He is not getting on very well since his wife left him.
8 She's very lucky as to get on so well with her parents.
9 Andrea got on that awful quiz programme last week and won a week in Torremolinos.
10 She's getting on a bit but she still goes skiing every winter.
11 It's getting on so I think we ought to stop now.

Hand your sentences to your teacher for checking.

Grammar

14 1 They **lived** in London for ten years and they left three years ago.
2 I **have been working** for the organisation Shelter since 1989.
3 Have you **seen** the latest Eric Rohmer film?
4 She **went** to Namibia three years ago.
5 George? No, sorry, he**'s** just **gone** out.
6 **Have** you ever **played** squash before or is this the first time?

15 Hand your sentences to your teacher for checking.

Writing

16 A Dangerous sports should be banned
For:
accidents always happen
protect people from themselves
expensive for the state
innocent people sometimes hurt
Against:
life too boring otherwise
hurt only themselves
people need to take risks
freedom of individual essential

B Regionalism is a dangerous phenomenon
For:
the whole is more than the sum of its parts
regionalism is a form of racism
regionalism leads to wars
regional parties have no sound national policies
Against:
national governments too far from people
some regions have been neglected by government
regionalism conserves regional culture
different regions have different mentalities

Unit 4

Vocabulary development

1 Hand your sentences to your teacher for checking.

Vocabulary building

2 bored boring qualified qualifying
amused amusing frightened frightening
depressed depressing thrilled thrilling

3 Hand your sentences to your teachers for checking.

Listening

4 1d 2b 3c 4d 5c 6b

5 Hand your summary to your teacher for checking.

Pronunciation

6 Check your answers by looking at the tapescript S9 .

Grammar

7 1 She**'s going to** have a baby in June.
2 I feel awful. I think I**'m going to** faint.
3 The last train **leaves** Euston at 11.30.
4 I**'ll help** with the washing up, if you like.
5 Claudia has missed her bus. She**'s going to** be late for work.

6 Chelsea have a very good side. I think they'**ll win** easily.
7 The referee is looking at his watch. He **is going to** blow his whistle.
8 They'**re meeting** me for dinner at eight o'clock this evening.
9 For most of 1995 he'**ll be visiting** the southern states of the USA.
10 It's six o'clock. They'**ll have arrived** in Kampala by now.

8 Hand your sentences to your teacher for checking.

Reading

9 1 Matmata   2 Ain Draham   3 Near Tunis
   4 Kerkennah   5 In the north   6 Dougga
   7 In the north   8 El Jem   9 Nefta/Tozeur
   10 Kairouan

10 (*Sample answers.*)
   1 That Tunisia is a bland mix of sunshine, beaches and a touch of the exotic.
   2 Because if you go beyond the beach resorts there are many interesting thins to see, such as the countryside, the monuments and the architecture.
   3 Antiquity, the spread of Islam in medieval times, the period of European and Turkish interest beginning in the fifteenth century, French colonisation, and twentieth-century independence.
   4 The scenery, the architecture, the monuments, the coast and the desert and mountains.
   5 Because local people are very friendly towards foreign visitors especially the independent traveller.
   6 The autumn.

Idioms

11 spit   It's spitting (with rain).
    tip   It's tipping down (with rain).
    chuck It's chucking it down.
    pour   It's pouring down (with rain).
    drizzle It's drizzling.
    pelt   It's pelting down (with rain).

Phrasal verbs

12 1 up 2 back 3 in 4 off 5 down 6 round 7 over 8 after 9 on 10 out

Hand your sentences to your teacher for checking.

Grammar

13 Known as Ceylon for several hundred years, the ancient name of Sri Lanka (**Resplendent** Land) has been restored. It is a **fitting** one, for this Indian Ocean Island – 25,000 square miles filled with a **great** variety of scenery and surrounded by **beautiful, palm-fringed** beaches – is a traveller's delight.

Journey inland from Colombo, the capital, and you will find scenic attractions, **natural** and **man-made** … the **cool, pleasant** hill country, swathed in the **dark** green of the tea estates, jungles, **vast** plains and **awe-inspiring** monuments to bygone civilisations.

Probably one of the most **memorable** features of your holiday will be the **delightful, friendly** people – always **welcoming** and **hospitable**. Hardly **surprising** then, that the word serendipity, the art of making **unexpected** and **pleasant** discoveries, is frequently used when speaking of this island paradise.

Writing

14 Hand your postcard to your teacher for checking.

Extension and consolidation

Editing

1 1 purpose-built 2 skiers 3 virtually 4 valley
   5 resorts 6 Although 7 modern 8 traditional
   9 whole 10 atmosphere 11 system 12 visitor
   13 prepared 14 skiing 15 challenging 16 for

Dictation

2 Check your answers by looking at the tapescript S10.

Extensive reading

3 (*Sample summary.*)
  Newby wrote this piece to express his disappointment about the way travelling was changing.

Unit 5

Vocabulary development

1 1 straightforward 2 standoffish 3 articulate
   4 approachable 5 argumentative 6 expressive

2 Hand your sentences to your teacher for checking.

Vocabulary building

3 1 off-limits 2 badly off 3 off-peak 4 comfortably off 5 off-season 6 off-form

4 Hand your sentences to your teacher for checking.

Listening

5 Conversation 1: 2, 4, 5, 7   Conversation 2: 1, 3, 6, 8

6 **Conversation 1**
  1 quid 2 guy 3 green 4 conned

  Conversation 2
  1 ripped off 2 tout 3 jump 4 mug

7 Hand your summaries to your teacher for checking.

Pronunciation

8 Check your answers by looking at the tapescript S12.

Reading

9 1 Parent 2 Adult 3 Child

10 1 Figure 3A 2 Figure 2A 3 Figure 2B

11 (*Sample answers.*)
   1 Stimulus: (Parent ego) Maybe we should find out why you've been drinking more lately.
     Response: (Child ego) You're always criticising me, just like my father did.
   2 Stimulus: (Adult ego) (Holds out hand for scalpel.)
     Response: (Adult ego) (Places handle of scalpel where expected.)
     or
     Stimulus: (Adult ego) Do you know where my cuff links are?
     Response: (Adult ego) On the desk.
   3 Stimulus: (Child ego) Can I have a drink of water?
     Response: (Parent ego) (Brings glass of water.)

Phrasal verbs

12 1 prising 2 fished 3 sniff 4 dig 5 fathom 6 spy

Grammar

13 1 getting 2 to play 3 to understand 4 to become
5 getting up 6 to learn 7 to cut 8 to tell
9 to interview 10 to go 11 to buy 12 cleaning

Improve your language learning

14 1H 2D 3F 4G 5I 6J 7K 8N 9A 10M 11B
12C 13L 14E

Text analysis

15 (*Sample paragraph.*) If you have found different grammatical features, hand your work to your teacher for checking.

Mundy led them sharply to the left, and Smiley guessed that by avoiding the centre of the village he hoped to escape the notice of the inhabitants. After about twenty minutes' walking, often through deep snow, they found themselves following a low hedge between two fields. In the furthest corner of the right-hand field they saw a pale light glimmering across the snow, so pale that at first Smiley had to look away from it then run his eyes back along the line of that distant hedge to make sure he was not deceived. Rigby stopped, beckoning to the others.

'I'll take over now,' he said. He turned to Smiley. 'I'd be obliged, sir, if you'd stand off a little. If there's any trouble, we don't want you mixed up in it, do we?'

Writing

15 Hand your letter to your teacher for checking.

Unit 6

Vocabulary development

1 1 **ancestors**: **ancestors** come before you whereas **offspring** and **descendants** come after you.
2 **child**: **brother** and **sister** are specific to one sex whereas a **child** can be of either sex.
3 **spouse**: a **spouse** can be a man or a woman whereas a **wife** and a **bride** can only be a woman.
4 **orphan**: an **orphan** has no parents whereas an **adopted child** and a **foster child** have acquired new ones.
5 **divorce**: to **divorce** is a legal act whereas to **separate** and to **split up** are more informal.
6 **parents**: **kin** and **relatives** describe anyone related to you whereas **parents** are specifically your mother and father.
7 **grow**: to **bring up** and to **raise** are transitive verbs describing the care and education of children whereas to **grow** is an intransitive verb. To **grow** can only be used transitively when referring to plants.

2 Give your paragraph to your teacher for checking.

Vocabulary building

3 (*Sample lists.*)

mother-in-law	stepmother
father-in-law	stepfather
sister-in-law	stepsister
brother-in-law	stepbrother
daughter-in-law	stepdaughter
son-in-law	stepson

Listening

4 1 As for the girl, she will **leave home** when she **gets married** and **goes off** to her in-laws.
2 ... when the boy **gets married**, his wife **comes home** and **lives with**, um, the in-laws.
3 We have to look after our parents because when ... it's like, when **we were kids** they **looked after us** and now we do the same when they **grow old**, we **look after** them.
4 No, she'll **move out when she** gets married.
5 Well, my mum and dad **gave me freedom when** I were young, so you know I **could go out by myself** to the shops and things like that ...
6 The Indian girls, they're **not really allowed** to go out.

Pronunciation

5 Check your answers by looking at the tapescript S14.

Grammar

6 (*Sample answers.*)
1 I wish people wouldn't park their cars in front of my garage.
2 I wish I hadn't eaten so much.
3 I wish she'd put the tops on bottles properly before putting them away.
4 I wish she could come to the concert.
5 I wish I hadn't spent so much at Christmas.
6 I wish they'd elected my party.
7 I wish we hadn't gone to Scotland.
8 I wish they'd be more considerate.

Reading

9 Advantages
Very good Christmases
Exciting lives compared to small families
Children well-balanced, optimistic and healthily competitive
Vitality and happiness of the mother

Disadvantages
Transport difficulties
High consumption of food
No privacy or space
Difficult to treat everyone fairly

Phrasal verbs

10 1b 2c 3a 4a 5c 6c 7a

Idioms

11 1 rose 2 daisies 3 thorn 4 weed 5 roses 6 daisy
7 nettled 8 grass

Grammar

12 1 be bought   2 is told   3 is invited
4 are, remembered   5 had been made   6 are, cheated
7 be taught

13 Hand your sentences to your teacher for checking.

Writing

14 His face was a very **strong** aquiline, with a **high** bridge of the **thin** nose and peculiarly arched nostrils; with lofty **domed** forehead, and hair growing scantily round the temples, but profusely elsewhere. His eyebrows were very **massive**, almost meeting over the nose, and with **bushy** hair that seemed to curl in its own profusion. The mouth, as far as I could see it under the **heavy** moustache, was fixed and rather **cruel-looking**, with peculiarly **sharp** white teeth; these protruded over the lips, whose remarkable ruddiness showed astonishing vitality in a man of his years. For the rest, his ears were pale and at the tops extremely **pointed**; the chin was **broad** and strong, and the cheeks firm though thin. The general effect was one of extraordinary pallor.

Hitherto I had noticed the backs of his hands as they lay on his knees in the firelight, and they had seemed rather white and **fine**; but seeing them now close to me, I could not but notice that they were rather coarse – **broad**, with squat fingers. Strange to say, there were hairs in the centre of the palm. The nails were **long** and fine, and cut to a sharp point.

The character is Dracula and the extract is from *Dracula* by Bram Stoker.

15 Hand your description to your teacher for checking.

Extension and consolidation

Editing

1 When she was about thirteen years old ~~the~~ her mother was taken ill, so the girl had to leave school for ~~the~~ good. She had her five young brothers and her father to look after, and there was ~~but~~ noone else to help ~~it~~. So she put away her books and her modest ambitions as she was naturally expected to do. The schoolmaster was ~~more~~ furious and called her father ~~as~~ a scoundrel but was helpless to interfere. 'Poor Mr Jolly,' said ~~the~~ Mother, fondly. 'He ~~was~~ never seemed to give up. He used to come round home when I was doing the washing and ~~he~~ lecture me on Oliver Cromwell. He used to sit there so sad, ~~by~~ saying it was a sinful shame, till Father ~~was~~ used to dance and swear …'

1 the 2 the 3 but 4 it 5 more
6 as 7 the 8 he 9 by 10 was

Dictation

2 Check your answers by looking at the tapescript S15.

Unit 7

Vocabulary development

1 1B 2A 3C 4C 5B 6A 7C 8B

Vocabulary building

2
List A
characterless
tactless
hopeless
powerless
lifeless

List B
countless
ageless
timeless
numberless

3 1 tactless 2 lifeless 3 timeless 4 ageless
5 characterless 6 hopeless

Listening

4 C
1 … a lot of people confuse it with **fashion** and you know what is fashionable to **wear** at the moment …
2 … I'm **not very** into smart cars **you know** and having all mod cons …
3 … to have a good lifestyle it's got to be all **fast** cars, **expensive** clothes and **rich** food …
4 … I don't need to spend **fifty pounds on a bottle of champagne**, that sort of thing …
5 … I don't like it when people try and impose their **style** on me …

Reading

7 A7 B2 C8 D6 E3 F9

Phrasal verbs

8 1 drop back 2 start back 3 think back 4 pay back
5 phone back 6 hold back 7 knock back

9 Hand your sentences to your teacher for checking.

Idioms

10 1D 2F 3A 4E 5C 6B

Grammar

11 The war to stop the rapidly spreading desert regions of the world is being met head-on by some nations. Israel's systematic pushing back of the desert with elaborate irrigation schemes and tree-planting are well-documented. Egypt and such places as Upper Volta are attempting to halt desert expansion by planting 'live fences': hedges of tough desert trees. Oil-rich Libya has come up with a bizarre scheme to stop expansion by paving the desert. Deep-rooted eucalyptus and acacia trees are planted on dunes. The dunes are sprayed with a layer of asphalt in order to stop the desert sands from shifting and burying the new trees.

One of the grandest schemes is the current construction of a 'Great Green Wall of China': a wall of living trees planted roughly parallel to that greatest of the planet's man-made structures, the ancient stone Great Wall. The Green Wall is designed to protect the nation from the invasion of cold winds and sandstorms that blast out of Siberia and Mongolia which have helped to create vast tracts of desert. The Green Wall is part of a massive reforestation plan which will result in the planting of over a quarter-million square miles of trees by the year 2000.

Writing

12 Hand your letter to your teacher for checking.

Unit 8

Vocabulary development

1 1 water 2 splash 3 loaded 4 thrifty 5 hard up 6 red
7 in 8 stingy 9 treats himself to 10 grasping

Vocabulary building

2 enjoyable imaginable identifiable variable
comfortable honourable valuable knowledgeable

3 Hand your sentences to your teacher for checking.

Listening

4 1, 2, 3, 5 and 7 apply to Denis.

5 (*Sample answers.*)
1 Denis comes from Doncaster in Yorkshire.
2 Because he was very young.
3 The very cold winters.
4 Because he used to sleep on the empty trains at Victoria Station and sometimes they were moved to Dover during the night.
5 He didn't make friends with them because he didn't trust them.
6 Through Sister Barbara at The Passage Day Centre.

Pronunciation
6 Check your answers by looking at the tapescript S19.

Grammar
7 2, 3, 4, 7, 9 and 10 are correct.
1 If you were to go down the High Street today, you **wouldn't** recognise it.
5 What **would** you do about unemployment if you were in the government?
6 Whether you **like** it or not, Michael Jackson is one of the greatest pop musicians in the world today.
8 Had they known that Miss Wimblesham was coming, they **would have sent** a car.

Reading
8 The writer of the article hates dogs.
A dog-lover wrote the letter (pretending to be a dog).

9 Dogs ...
1 are not intelligent
2 smell
3 make a mess of footpaths and roads
4 are often vicious
5 are very noisy
6 take up a lot of room
7 are over-affectionate
8 are expensive to keep
9 are ineffective at doing what they are trained to do

10 (*Sample list.*)
Dogs don't spoil the environment.
They don't rob, steal or rape.
They give pleasure to millions of people.
They can be used to locate dangerous drugs.

Idioms
11 Genuine expressions Slang expressions
cost a small fortune cost a packet
cost a mint cost a bomb
cost a packet
cost a bomb

Phrasal verbs
12 1D 2E 3F 4G 5C 6B 7A

13 1 holding 2 chanced 3 dotes 4 turned
5 counting 6 cheered 7 expanded

Grammar
14 1 So beautiful was the painting that I wanted to buy it.
or Such was the beauty of the painting that I wanted to buy it.
2 Hardly had I left the building when it started to rain.
3 No sooner had I stepped into the bath than the doorbell rang.
4 Not only does Kathy work as a teacher but she also writes children's fiction.
5 So fat is my cat, Elvis, that he can no longer get in through the cat flap.
6 Never have I made such an interesting journey.
7 Only when I drove off did I notice the flat tyre.
8 Under no circumstances will I do overtime unless you pay me double the hourly rate.

Writing
15 Hand your story to your teacher for checking.

Extension and consolidation
Editing
1
> Dear John,
>
> Yesterday I went to a job inteview in South Kensington. When I left the weather was awful. It was pouring with rain, and the wind was blowing cold and hard.
>
> I walked to the tube but when I came to buy my ticket I had no money. I had lost it.
>
> The only way home was to walk. I came out of the tube, about to start walking in the rain, and asked the guy who sells The Big Issue outside the station which way it was to Oxford Street. He realised my misfortune and dug in his pocket and gave me a pound, enough to get me home.
>
> I'd just like to say that I do buy The Big Issue in aid of helping the homeless and I am stunned that, when the tables were turned, someone less fortunate than myself was eager to help.
>
> Thanks to the guy from South Kensington.
>
> Yours sincerely,
>
> Soraya

Dictation
2 Check your answers by looking at the tapescript S20.

Extensive reading
3 (*Sample summary.*)
The narrator is describing his depression and fear, which have led to vivid flights of imagination.

Unit 9
Vocabulary development
1 Hand your sentences to your teacher for checking.

Vocabulary building
2 people painter farmer waiter photographer manager objects cooker recorder duster mixer blender

(*Sample definitions.*)

painter an artist who paints pictures; a person whose job is painting the walls, doors and windows, and so on, of buildings
farmer a person who owns or manages a farm
waiter a man who works in a restaurant serving people with food and drink
photographer a person who takes photographs for a living
cooker a large item of kitchen equipment used for cooking food, powered by oil, gas or electricity
blender a small item of kitchen equipment used for mixing foods together into a smooth liquid substance
duster a cloth used for removing dust from furniture, ornaments, and so on
recorder a musical instrument, belonging to the flute family; short for **tape recorder**, a machine for playing and recording onto cassettes
mixer a machine used for mixing things together, for example **food mixer, cement mixer**

Phrasal verbs

3 1 run away   keep away   5 melt away   wear away
   2 take away   call away   6 slog away   work away
   3 clear away   tuck away
   4 explain away wash away

4 Hand your sentences to your teacher for checking.

Listening

5 Hand your description to your teacher for checking.

Pronunciation

6 Check your answers by looking at the tapescript S22.

Reading

8 6 Ms Parrott says she cannot afford to be materialistic.
   4 So they sold everything and bought a narrowboat.
   1 'I don't mind if people glance through the window,' says Tricia Parrott, looking out at the path alongside her home.
   7 'It's like living in a linear village,' she says.
   5 What most people might mind about Ms Parrott's way of life is the inconvenience.
   3 What she and her husband gave up 20 years ago was a two-bedroom flat in Holland Park, west London.
   2 Ms Parrott, 57, has lived on the barge for eight years (alone, for the past two, since the death of her husband, Eric, a schoolteacher) and for 12 years before that on a narrowboat on the same mooring.

9 (*Sample answers.*)
   1 Canals are romantic.
   2 Living on a houseboat is mentally relaxing.
   3 Because of the magic of it all, the light shining off the water and reflected on the roof, the freedom, the camaraderie.
   4 Things are always busy and happening and she has a network of friends.
   5 The water is very soothing.

Idioms

10 1 chicken 2 duck 3 duck 4 crowing 5 lark
    6 chickens 7 crow 8 lark

Grammar

11 2 won't you?
    3 hasn't he?
    4 aren't you?
    6 shall I?

(*Sample answers.*)
   1 Yes, you are./No, you're not actually.
   2 Yes, I will.
   3 Yes, he has./Not really.
   4 Yes, it's not bad.
   5 No, I don't actually.
   6 OK, go on then.
   7 Yes, of course.
   8 No, you can count on me.
   9 Yes, I did.
  10 Yes, all right. It looks fine.

12 Hand your questions to your teacher for checking.

13 1 Bristol is a busy university city which is in the west of England.
    2 This is Alison, whose boat I lived on this summer.
    3 I spent all my money which annoyed my wife enormously.
    4 There was a group of football supporters on our train, one of whom jumped out while the train was still moving.
    5 For our holidays we are going to Galicia, which is in the north-west of Spain.
    6 For Christmas they gave me three cassettes, of which I already had two.
    7 Chet Baker, who was a famous jazz trumpet player, died last year.

14 1 Have the police found the car **that was stolen**?
    2 I didn't really enjoy the new record **that I heard last week**.
    3 Have you seen the interesting painting **that we bought on holiday**?
    4 The bicycle **that was vandalised outside the school** belongs to the new French teacher.
    5 This is one of the photographs **that Robert Capa took in 1942**.
    6 The doctor's secretary, **who came to the door**, told me the doctor was out.
    7 You shouldn't believe all the gossip **you hear in the canteen**.

Writing

15 Hand your composition to your teacher for checking.

Unit 10

Vocabulary development

1 Check your answers on page 73 of your Students' Book, and hand your sentences to your teacher for checking.

2 Hand your sentences to your teacher for checking.

Vocabulary building

3 (*Sample answers.*)

   1 bluish white   4 reddish purple
   2 bluish black   5 brownish red
   3 greeny yellow   6 maroony purple

Hand your adjective-noun combinations to your teacher for checking.

Listening

4 1 and 6 are false.
2, 3, 4, 5 and 7 are true.

5 1 I don't think I tend to **get depressed for very long**.
2 I mean, like my girlfriend **gets depressed sometimes**.
3 I wouldn't know how to deal with it **if it was a sort of clinical depression or they really got seriously depressed**.
4 I remember living with **one guy at university** ... **he was depressed all the time**.
5 Yeah, I don't think **I ever saw him happy**.

Idioms

6 (*Sample definitions*.)

1 very keen to hear the details of what happened next
2 listening very hard to something that is being said even though it has nothing to do with one
3 the information given is forgotten immediately
4 make sure one is well informed about other people's opinions and activities
5 thrown out suddenly and unpleasantly
6 a punch or slap on the side of the head
7 taken no notice of
8 completely absorbed with paperwork to the exclusion of all else

Pronunciation

7 Check your answers by looking at the tapescript S23 on page 85.

Reading

8 (*Sample answers*.)

1 To reveal the conscious and unconscious psychological structure of the individual, areas of psychic stress, the state of glandular balance or imbalance and other physiological information.
2 Looking at and ordering a series of colours.
3 Doctors and psychotherapists.

9 (*Sample sentences*.)

1 We choose colours according to circumstances and aesthetic considerations.
2 People doing the test should select the colours just as colours, without making associations with objects or paying any attention to how the colours look together.
3 It requires specialist knowledge to interpret the full Lüscher colour test, which contains 73 colour patches.
4 The short Lüscher Test, which contains only eight colours, is less thorough than the full test but is easier to administer.
5 The test can be used as an 'early warning system' by physicians to give early indications of street-related physical problems such as heart disease and digestive disorders.
6 The Short Lüscher Test is useful for the busy doctor who can delegate his or her nurse to administer it and then check the results him or herself.

Phrasal verbs

10 1 in 2 up 3 off 4 around 5 through 6 up 7 up
8 around

Grammar

11 Wrong verbs are used in Sentences 1, 2, 4, 6, 7, 9 and 10.

1 He didn't have a car so he **can't** have driven home.
2 This isn't Conkreton, we **must** have taken the wrong road.
4 A week after he had the operation he **was able to** return to work.
6 **Would/Could** you give me an envelope, please?
7 They **didn't need to** plan their holiday last year because their parents booked everything for them.
9 They **might/may** be coming to the party, but I'm not sure.
10 You **can/may** go home early today, if you want to.

12 Hand your sentences to your teacher for checking.

13 Hand your guide to your teacher for checking.

Extension and consolidation

Editing

1 1 I used * think white is white is white. But as with every other colour,
2 there are dozens of different shades. And I've come * realise that the
3 warmer tones * my favourites.
4 In saying this, I'm influenced by * latest trends. The creamy white of
5 unbleached cotton and the powdery bloom of stone * big news in
6 decorating, thanks to our growing preference for simplicity * natural materials. But
7 it also feels right. Just as there are days * only a snowy white shirt
8 will do, so * are times when it's the only colour I'm prepared to consider
9 when I look * towels or china.
10 However there * nothing faddy about decorating with warm whites. On
11 the contrary, I can't think of * more timeless approach. Freeing yourself from
12 anxieties * surround colour (What if I hate it? How will it look on
13 a dreary winter's day?) gives you a chance * escape the tyranny of
14 decorating trends. You * longer have to worry about splashy wallpapers
15 looking dated * two years' time, or whether you'll be able to live with
16 lime green upholstery for the rest * your days.

1 to 2 to 3 are 4 the 5 are 6 and 7 when
8 there 9 for 10 is 11 a 12 that 13 to
14 no 15 in 16 of

Dictation

2 Check your answers by looking at the tapescript S25.

Improve your language learning

3 1A 2C 3H 4J 5F 6D 7I 8B 9E
4 A,B,C 6 A,G 2 I,F 3 H,J 4 D,H 5 F
6 B 7 F,I 8 C,G 9 I 10 B

These are the authentic versions of the three fake texts identified in Exercise 4.

Nag Hammadi
At NAG HAMMADI, 40km from Abydos and 560km from Cairo, the Nile sweeps eastwards into the 'Qena Bend' and the main road and railway transfer from the west bank to the eastern side of the river. Nag Hammadi itself is an important agricultural centre whose Nile barrage irrigates over 622,000 *feddans*, though there's nothing here to attract tourists save for the *Aluminium Hotel* (757-947), 7km south of town. This is probably the most comfortable **accommodation** between Assyut and Luxor (singles £E30, doubles £E40) and might come in handy if more distant options prove impractical.

Precautions

- Do not use this product if you have an allergy to any of its contents.
- Do not take tablets internally.
- Do not place HYDROCARE™ FIZZY protein remover tablet solution or LC-65™ directly into your eyes and do not insert lenses directly from the weekly protein remover solution. Rinse and disinfect (overnight storage) first.
- Do not leave low water content soft or gas permeable contact lenses in protein remover solution for longer than 12 hours.
- Do not soak high water content lenses in protein remover solution for more than 2 hours.
- DO NOT MIX WITH OTHER FLUIDS EXCEPT AS DIRECTED.
- Store at room temperature. Avoid excessive heat.
- Keep out of the reach of children.
- If eye irritation occurs, discontinue lens wear and consult your contact lens practitioner.
- Consult your practitioner before using this product concurrently with other eye medications.

+ at 4.15, 8.35: **'Barton Fink'** (15) (Joel and Ethan Coen, 1991, US) John Turturro, John Goodman, Judy Davis, Michael Lerner. A well-meaning, vaguely leftist Broadway playwright (Turturro) tries to settle into a rancid hotel room, to write his first Hollywood script. Trouble is, he has no idea what to put in a lowly wrestling pic and develops a severe case of writer's block. His only hope, it seems, is to take inspiration from writer Mayhew's secretary Audrey (Davis) and from his insurance salesman neighbour Charlie Meadows (Goodman). The tortuous narrative twists that have always marked the Coens' work here inform the movie's entire structure. As it suddenly shifts gear from its blend of brooding psychodrama and screwball satire, the film accelerates into a Gothic fantasy as outrageous as it is terrifying. Somehow everything coheres, thanks to superb writing and assured direction, and a roster of marvellous performances.

Unit 11

Vocabulary development

1 (*Sample answers.*)

1 **textbook** a **textbook** contains facts; **comedies** and **thrillers** are fiction.
2 **fable** a **fable** is a story; **manuals** and **atlases** are reference books.
3 **intriguing** **hilarious** and **witty** both mean funny.
4 **poem** a **poem** is always written in verse form; **sagas** and **fables** my be prose or verse.
5 **short story** a **short story** is fiction; **biographies** and **textbooks** are factual.
6 **bold** **profound** and **deep** have the same meaning.
7 **plod through** **leaf through** and **skip through** mean to read very quickly.
8 **plodding** **inane** and **crass** both mean silly.

Vocabulary building

2 ambiguous famous
 cautious religious
 courageous mysterious
 curious spontaneous

3 1 courageous 2 spontaneous 3 mysterious 4 famous
 5 ambiguous 6 curious 7 religious 8 cautious

Listening

4 an international holiday resort
 a logging camp
 a woollen mill in Yorkshire
 a lawyer's office in London
 a sheep station in New Zealand
 a factory in England

5 1, 5 and 6 are false.
 2, 3, 4 and 7 are true.

Pronunciation

6 Check your answer by looking at the tapescript S27.

Reading

7 B

8 A7 B5 C1 D3 E8 F6 G2 H4

Phrasal verbs

9 A3 B1 C5 D4 E2

10 (*Sample sentences.*)

1 The council really disagreed with the government's decision to build a by-pass but they eventually had to give way.
2 When I heard that our cat had been run over I gave way to tears.
3 When you come up to a junction and there is a solid white line on the road, you have to give way to cars on the other road.
4 Although the sky was full of grey thunder clouds in the morning, later in the day they gave way to blue skies and sunshine.
5 Thirty people who had been working on the second floor of the building were seriously injured when the floor gave way.

Idioms

11 (*Sample explanations.*)

1 **tongue-tied** confused and embarrassed to the point of being unable to speak
2 **tongue-twister** a sentence or expression which is very difficult to say quickly
3 **hold one's tongue** keep quiet, not say anything
4 **lose one's tongue** be unable to speak (often used in annoyance or sarcastically, similar to the cat's got your tongue)
5 **get one's tongue round** find something difficult to pronounce
6 **a slip of the tongue** a mistake, used when you say something you didn't mean to say

Grammar

12 Hand your sentences to your teacher for checking.

Writing

13 Hand your composition to your teacher for checking.

Unit 12

Vocabulary development

1 Hand your paragraph to your teacher for checking.

Vocabulary building

2 imaginative attractive productive protective
 creative decisive conclusive offensive

93

3 Hand your sentences to your teacher for checking.

Reading

4 Eric Clapton

5 1d 2e 3a 4f 5b 6c

Idioms

6 1a 2c 3b 4a

Phrasal verbs

7 1 down 2 out of 3 up 4 in 5 back 6 at 7 from 8 to

Listening

8 (*Sample answers.*)

1 She enjoyed her primary education most. The pupils were from a variety of social backgrounds, the school was in her village and they had a good teacher who made them feel secure.
2 The school was in another town, the pupils were all girls, the teachers were very strict and the classroom didn't bear much resemblance to real life.
3 It was 1968 when politics were top of the agenda. If you weren't committed politically, you were out of it.
4 They just gave lessons and didn't get involved in their students' lives and general development.
5 There were only twenty people on her course.
6 It has left her with an idea of what to do and what not to do in class now that she is a teacher herself.
7 It goes on in an atmosphere of greater tolerance and freedom and is more interesting.

Pronunciation

9 Check your answers by looking at the tapescript S29 .

Grammar

10 Hand your summary to your teacher for checking.

(*Sample summary.*)

Evie asked her friend about a picture of Drumstrings Casey and her friend told her she had done it at a place called the Unicorn. She asked Evie if she thought it was a good likeness. Evie wanted to know how her friend had done the drawing and her friend told her about the Unicorn. Her friend asked her if she had ever been to the Unicorn but Evie had to admit that she had never heard of it. Her friend offered to take her there the following Saturday when Drumstrings Casey would be playing and Evie accepted the invitation. Her friend gave her the picture and was surprised that Evie thought she wanted something in return for it.

Writing

11 Hand your letter to the your teacher for checking.

Extension and consolidation

Editing

1 In the home the child is always being taught. In almost every home there is always at least one ungrown-up grown-up who rushes to show Tommy how his engine works. There is always someone to lift the baby up on a chair when baby wants to examine something on the wall. Every time we show Tommy how his engine works we are stealing from that child the joy of life – the joy of discovery – the joy of overcoming an obstacle. Worse! We make that child come to believe that he is inferior and must depend on help.

Parents are slow in realizing how unimportant the learning side of school is. Children, like adults, learn what they want to learn. All prize-giving and marks and exams sidetrack proper personality development. Only pedants claim that learning from books is education.

Dictation

2 Check your answers by looking at the tapescript S30 .

Unit 13

Vocabulary development

1 Hand your review to your teacher for checking.

Vocabulary building

2 alcoholic nationalistic photographic democratic artistic moralistic enthusiastic pessimistic ironic poetic

3 Hand your sentences to your teacher for checking.

Phrasal verbs

4 (*Sample sentences.*)

1 It was very cold out so he put up the collar of his jacket.
2 The sweep put his brush up the chimney to clean it.
3 She put up the painting on the wall next to the window.
4 I put up my umbrella when it started raining.
5 He put up a good fight in the World Boxing Championship.
6 She put up a proposal to ban smoking at the meeting.
7 The government put up the price of beer in the annual budget.
8 I put them up in my flat for three days.
9 Her party put her up as a candidate in the last election.

Idioms

5 (*Sample definitions.*)

1 **be all eyes** be very observant and looking all around eagerly
2 **run one's eye over something** look or glance quickly at something
3 **catch someone's eye** attract someone's attention
4 **have one's eye on someone** watch and make judgements about someone
5 **keep one's eyes peeled** constantly watch
6 **keep an eye on someone or something** watch and take care of someone or something
7 **make eyes at someone** look at someone in a way that indicates that you are attracted to them
8 **more to something than meets the eye** something is more complicated than it originally appeared to be
9 **see eye to eye with someone** agree with and share views with someone, and get on well with them
10 **up to one's eyes in something** very busy with something so that you have no time to spare

Pronunciation

6 Check your answers by looking at the tapescript S31 .

Listening

7 1 **The Ritz** most modern cinema in Richmond, bulldozed in sixties, office block
The Gaumont scruffiest cinema in Richmond, nicknamed the 'flea pit', demolished in seventies, façade remains, offices
The Odeon most beautiful cinema in Richmond, now three-screen cinema, architecture intact
The Conway cinema in Aberystwyth
The Cambrian cinema in Aberystwyth where *Ben Hur* anecdote took place
The Celtic cinema in Aberystwyth

2 *The Comancheros* was the first film he remembers seeing. He gives *Pipe-laying in Siberia* as an example of the obscure short films that were shown in the Cambrian before the main film and during which the students used to shout out funny comments. He was watching *Ben Hur* for the first time at the Cambrian when the ceiling fell down on the front three rows of the audience.

3 As a student he worked at a supermarket. The supermarket was closed on Mondays. None of his friends were around on Mondays so he would go to the cinema twice, once in the afternoon and once in the evening.

4 A section of the ceiling fell down on the front three rows of the audience.

Reading

8 A7 B10 C4 D1 E5 F9 G8 H3 I2 J6

Grammar

9 1 I sat in the living room reading a book until our friends arrived.
2 Being fluent in three languages, Betty and her husband are often invited to parties at the embassy.
3 When we were in Milan last week we saw many children begging in the streets.
4 Having put the car in the garage, Wendy went into the house.
5 The bell rang and when I opened the door there was a group of children singing.
6 On Thursday my sister turned up at my house wearing a bright red evening dress.
7 Having lost my ticket, I had to pay again when the inspector came round.
8 Arriving at the airport two hours before the flight, we went and had lunch.

Writing

10 Hand your letter or composition to your teacher for checking.

Unit 14

Vocabulary development

1 1 sketch 2 landscape 3 masterpiece 4 still life 5 abstract 6 reproduction 7 portrait 8 drawing 9 ink

2 1 ink 2 abstract 3 reproduction 4 sketch 5 drawing 6 masterpiece 7 portrait 8 landscape 9 still life

Vocabulary building

3 Category 1 dockside trackside lakeside seaside roadside
Category 2 passenger-side farside underside
Category 3 aside inside reside alongside

Pronunciation

4 Check your answers by looking at the tapescript S33.

Listening

5 (*Sample answers.*)

His three main responsibilities Director of the Hayward Gallery Responsible for touring exhibitions programme Curator of the Arts Council collection
Current exhibitions at the Hayward Gallery Mexican Art on the ground floor Bridget Riley's abstract paintings upstairs
Weak points of the Gallery space not very flexible – can only be divided into two areas, downstairs and upstairs – whole Gallery has to be closed down between exhibitions
Future plans for the Gallery possibly rebuild it

Reading

6 Goya Degas Van Gogh Palmer Matisse Renoir Sisley Feininger Nolde Munch

7 1, 3, 6 and 8 are false.
2, 4, 5, 7, 9 and 10 are true.

1 People thought he was crazy when he made his claims about receiving inspiration from the great painters.
3 He wasn't ill, he went into a sort of trance.
6 He wrote messages on the canvas which, when X-rayed, would show up, thereby proving the painting to be a forgery.
8 The dealers didn't necessarily pay attention to the date of the paper. They seemed to want to believe that a painting was genuine and so paid attention to the messages on the back.

Phrasal verbs

8 1 on/down 2 over 3 up 4 between 5 on 6 out 7 off 8 round

9 Hand your sentences to your teacher for checking.

Idioms

10 (*Sample definitions.*)

1 **put everything one has into something** use all one's energy to do something
2 **be had up for** appear in court for a crime
3 **have had it** to be worn out, beyond repair
4 **have it in for someone** be determined to cause unpleasantness for someone
5 **have it in one** have the ability or skill to do something
6 **have it out** talk openly to someone about something you disagree on

Grammar

11 Hand your sentences to your teacher for checking.

(*Sample sentences.*)

1 When I was younger I worked as a postman in my Christmas holidays.

2 Your face is red. You look like a lobster.
3 He had to go to hospital as his wife had had an accident.
4 I really like modern music, like *The Red Hot Chillie Peppers*.
5 I was late for the concert and I got there as they were closing the doors.
6 Where's Andrew? Oh! That sounds like him now.
7 The news of her promotion came as a great surprise.
8 When I left they gave me a cake as big as a house.

Writing

12 Hand your dialogue to your teacher for checking.

Extension and consolidation

Editing

1 On an aeroplane you're helpless. The film you're see is somebody else's choice, and it usually has the George Segal in it. Once I watched a whole of movie with the wrong soundtrack. It was *Fletch*, and when Chevy Chase spoke it was Julie Andrews who came from out of his mouth. You're trapped in the your headphones and trapped in your seat. You feel helpless, too, because you're watching at it in danger. Cinemas are safe, that it is one of their charms. They're dark and upholstered and warm as the womb. There are staff with the uniforms to look after of you. A plane cabin tries to fool you with the same set-up, but suddenly it meets a turbulence, bumps and jolts, and three hundred of you are sit there thinking of the drop beneath. In the middle of *A Man for all the Seasons* there's a ping, and on come the little red signs: FASTEN YOUR SEATBELTS. In the front of the celluloid swordfight are three hundred souls fear for their lives.

Dictation

2 Check your answers in the tapescript S35.